The Gift of Encouragement

To Flo —
All grace and joy
in the encouragement
of the Spirit!

Majorie J. Thompson

Praise for *The Gift of Encouragement*

The Gift of Encouragement is itself a gift of encouragement. The ancient experience of "losing heart" is widespread in our era, so this book on "restoring heart" is both ageless and timely. As Marjorie Thompson has shown us time and again in her writing, she is deeply grounded in Christian faith, and is able to articulate that faith with a clarity and grace that help us bring belief to life. She understands that God does not "fix" us but walks with us in compassion—and she shows us how to incarnate that good news with those who suffer. May this book be read by many, and may they become companions on the journey to many, many more.

—Parker J. Palmer, author of *Healing the Heart of Democracy*, *The Courage to Teach*, and *Let Your Life Speak*

Marjorie Thompson's uplifting and compelling book about the gift of encouragement is itself a gift and an encouragement. Designed as a guide for caregivers who work with those who have lost heart, the book is a means of encouragement to both care-receivers and caregivers. Filled with practical exericses, realistic cases, and beautiful prayers, Thompson offers us a wealth of resources to foster encouragenent in our lives and the lives of others.

—Rebekah Miles, Perkins School of Theology, Southern Methodist University

Marjorie Thompson offers the gift of encouragement at a time and in a culture that desperately needs that gift. Who of us cannot identify with the need for encouragement in our troubled and anxious world? MarjorieThompson has written a book that will be of great benefit to everyone who has ever found it hard to forgive or who has felt less than worthwhile. It is a resource that I will use and give to those who hunger for some faithful word of encouragement and who long to be in a closer relationship with God.

—Rueben Job, retired United Methodist bishop, former World Editor of The Upper Room, and author

The Gift of Encouragement

Restoring Heart to
Those Who Have Lost It

Marjorie J. Thompson

Abingdon Press
Nashville, Tennessee

This book is printed on acid-free paper.

Library of Congress Cataloging-in-Publication Data has been requested.

ISBN 978-1-4267-4419-8

Scripture quotations unless noted otherwise are from the Common English Bible. Copyright © 2011 by the Common English Bible. All rights reserved. Used by permission. www.CommonEnglishBible.com.

Scripture quotations marked (NRSV) are taken from the New Revised Standard Version of the Bible, copyright 1989, Division of Christian Education of the National Council of the Churches of Christ in the United States of America. Used by permission. All rights reserved.

The Emotional Health Self-Assessment on pp. 50–53 and 98–100 is taken from Peter Scazzero, *Emotionally Healthy Spirituality* (Nashville: Thomas Nelson, 2006). Reprinted with permission.

13 14 15 16 17 18 19 20 21 22—10 9 8 7 6 5 4 3 2 1

MANUFACTURED IN MEXICO

To the parishioners of Trinity Presbyterian Church,
Hendersonville, NC;
First Presbyterian Church, Stamford, CT;
and my spiritual directees over the years,
all of whom have taught me so much

CONTENTS

INTRODUCTION

As ordinary mortals, even the most persistent optimists among us become discouraged at times. To be discouraged means to lose heart. Metaphorically and spiritually, the heart is the core of human energy, emotional connection, and drive for life. When we lose heart, we may become bored and restless with life, fearful of the future and anxious in the present, cynical about people or institutions, passive or distant in our relationships, and low on basic energy for daily tasks. We may even descend into the profound isolation of depression. Sources of discouragement seem endless. Perhaps we experience failure at some endeavor, or a person we trusted betrays us. A sudden loss changes our lives forever, a dreaded diagnosis is given, or a new perspective on reality shakes the foundations of our faith. Perhaps we feel our elected officials have failed us, our public social structures are crumbling, or that "the system" is rigged against us. Sometimes it seems life is just a series of curve balls in a game where survival requires a constant dance of repositioning ourselves to maintain any sense of balance or stability.

What resources from our faith tradition can

offer the gift of encouragement, a restoring of heart to those who have lost it? In the pages that follow, I hope to suggest perspectives and practices that might help wobbly legs find a sense of solid ground underfoot. Solid ground gives a place to stand, to recover balance, to rest and be replenished. The familiar biblical image of God as "rock" suggests the kind of solidity and firmness we seek when our heads are spinning from the changing challenges of life. As we get "grounded in God," we discover the gifts of reorientation and renewed strength. Our spirits are filled; our hearts come back to life; our courage returns.

This book is written for all who have concern and care for discouraged people in their lives and ministries. I trust it will also speak to the discouragement we know at times within ourselves. From common human experience we empathize with fellow journeyers struggling with loss of heart. I believe the image of God in which we are created includes great generosity of heart, supplying each of us with a profound reserve of courage. Helping one another rediscover the gift of courage residing deep within is part of our calling as followers of Jesus. It offers us a way of maturing in Christ's love. As a pastor and spiritual guide, I have always found it a great privilege and honor to accompany others on this journey into the fullness of what God yearns for us to be! I trust you have found or will find it to be so as well.

We will explore four basic areas about which we commonly feel discouraged: our selves, our work, our relationships, and our spiritual lives. In relation to these, we will consider Scripture texts, spiritual practices, and words of wisdom from Christian tradition that could help reorient those suffering from discouragement. The areas explored here are by no means exhaustive, but rather suggestive of types of situations we might face in helping others. Neither are the practices suggested comprehensive, but chosen to suit the kinds of situations described here.

In our encouraging of others, we do not want to imply that the goal or norm of human life is to get past all suffering. Jesus tells his disciples before his death, "In the world you have distress. But be encouraged! I have conquered the world" (John 16:33). Julian of Norwich, fourteenth-century anchoress and mystic, reflects on this truth: "He did not say: You will not be troubled, you will not be belaboured, you will not be disquieted; but he said: You will not be overcome."[1]

Life on earth involves us in suffering—our own and that of others. This is only natural in a finite world where life and death weave a constant dance. The simple truth is that we do not grow—physically, emotionally, or spiritually—without encountering, coping with, and learning from suffering. Certainly we learn far more from experiences that push us out of our comfort zones than from a life of smooth sailing. And as most of us discover, we cannot become truly empathetic or compassionate toward others if we have not known loss and hardship ourselves. Saint John of Kronstadt (nineteenth century) wisely counseled: "Do not fear the conflict, and do not flee from it; where there is no struggle, there is no virtue. Our faith, trust, and love are proved and revealed in adversities, that is, in difficult and grievous outward and inward circumstances, during sickness, sorrow, and privations."[2]

In the spiritual life, without suffering there can be no maturing into the fullness of our humanity. The way of the cross entails dying to our small, ego-centered life so that we may rise into our true selfhood—the identity that finds its center and ground in God. This true human identity is represented and fully embodied in Christ, "the image of the invisible God" (Col. 1:15). We, too, are created in the divine image, and as believers we are promised the destiny of being conformed to Christ (Rom. 8:29), in whom we recover the beauty and clarity of that image.

Whereas I do not believe God actively creates suffering for us, surely God allows us to undergo adversities with a continual hope that we will open up to the very real transformations they can work in us if we are willing. The questions we ask of one another and of ourselves in times of trial are important: What are you learning from this experience? How does it enlarge your view of life, of others, of yourself? Is there an invitation from God within this experience that is new or surprising to you—or perhaps urging you further toward something you already know? These are questions aimed at evoking our deeper wisdom and guidance from the Spirit dwelling within.

Nothing of our life's experience is lost or wasted when we are open to grace—even if we have made terrible choices, affecting our lives and the lives of others for years; even if we bear and inflict permanent scars; even if we have lost years of productive work to chronic illness or depression; even if our life seems the most boring, meaningless existence possible. The Holy One takes it all into the immense humility of Christ for the repair and replenishing that only love can fashion. "The Ascension is Christ's return to the heart of all creation....Faith reveals that Christ, dwelling at the center of all creation and of each individual member of it, is transforming it and bringing it back, in union with himself, into the bosom of the Father."[3]

God has promised to use our life experiences in ways that build toward a new configuration of goodness: "We know that God works all things together for good for the ones who love God"

(Rom. 8:28). No matter what kind of mess we find ourselves in or create by our thoughtless distraction or willful rebellion, God continues the long, patient process of reweaving our broken threads into a new tapestry. This seems to be the divine job description: making heavenly gold out of human lead. Of course, God can do even more with our willing cooperation, since this is what we are created for!

What a powerful source of hope and encouragement this offers to us all. The great promises of our faith are incalculable gifts to those who believe them:

- God is with us always. (Josh. 1:5, 9; Matt. 28:20)

- Love, life, and light lie at the heart of all creation. (John 1:1-5; Eph. 1:9-10, 22-23; Col. 1:15-17)

- There is no need to be afraid. (Luke 2:9–11; 12:6-7, 32; 24:36-39; Matt. 6:25-33, 28:5-10; 1 John 4:18)

- The Spirit is within, and will guide us as we listen. (1 Cor. 6:19; John 14:25-26)

- The blessed life is to be found in God's way: simplicity, humility, right relationships, mercy, purity, and peace. (Matt. 5:3-9)

- Peace and joy are the gifts of life in Christ. (John 14:27; 15:11; Eph. 2:14)

- The end of life on earth is but the beginning of something wonderfully new in God's eternal reality. (John 14:1-3; 2 Cor. 4:16–5:5)

Our faith proclaims that ultimately God will prevail, unconditional love will reveal its fullness, the New Creation will manifest in glory, and—as Julian of Norwich saw in one of her revelations and put so memorably to words—"Sin is necessary, but all will be well, and all will be well, and every kind of thing will be well."[4] This is our deep faith, our realistic hope, and the source, sustenance, and destiny of our love. What greater encouragement could we hope for?

CHAPTER 1

The Courage of Authentic Self-Love

One of the deepest forms of discouragement human beings can experience revolves around a personal sense of self. When people don't feel good about who they are, those feelings negatively influence virtually every relationship—with work, others, and God.

There are many people who have not actually received much by way of love or affirmation in their lives. They often feel small, unimportant, "not good enough" in the eyes of the world. Perhaps they struggled to achieve in school. Perhaps they received more criticism than praise for their best efforts. Their parents may have been emotionally immature—preoccupied and distant, or demanding and punitive. Many people of solid character and virtue have experienced being ignored or overlooked for those who seem more gifted or charismatic. Those in positions of authority often underappreciate modest but steady gifts and skills.

During thirty years in ministry, I have learned that even people who seem highly successful and self-confident can suffer a basic lack of self-esteem, most often rooted in their early history with family and school. True self-esteem is not egocentrism but a capacity for healthy self-respect and realistic self-confidence. It could be called authentic love of self. In the Great Commandment, alongside wholehearted love of God, Jesus says, "Love your neighbor as you love yourself" (Matt. 22:39). One writer has wryly noted, "If you do a bad job of loving yourself, your neighbor is not going to benefit much from that formula."[1] For in addition to those who have not in fact received much love, countless people have difficulty allowing themselves to receive love—either from God or others—and consequently have trouble loving themselves.

Those who lack healthy self-esteem are not well equipped to esteem others in healthy ways either. They are likely to idealize the gifts and capacities of others while denigrating their own, or to judge others harshly as a way to deflect and disguise how they despise themselves. These are mostly unconscious behaviors. When you observe persons habitually criticizing others, face-to-face or behind their backs, you can be certain they do not feel good about themselves. Likewise, when people praise others and demean themselves, you can see their impoverished sense of self.

Deep-seated lack of self-esteem is related to a pervasive sense of shame. Shame differs significantly from guilt. Guilt is related to *what we do* or fail to do, whereas shame is related to our sense of *who we are*. When shame grips us, it is not so much our actions that condemn us, but somehow our very being. Children who are perceived by other children as different in any way are often ostracized, excluded, or bullied in school. Perhaps they are considered unattractive; have physical or learning impairments; represent a culture, faith, or sexual orientation differing from the majority; or are simply introverted and shy. These children are at risk for developing a sense of shame about who they are by virtue of traits they have little or no control over.

I have observed parents repeatedly tell their children that they are bad boys or girls. These parents do not think to distinguish between person and behavior. The message their children hear is not that what they have *done* is bad, but that they *themselves* are bad. Such children are likely to suffer pervasive, unconscious shame. Children with healthy self-esteem can sometimes articulate the difference between doing and being. A woman once told me of an incident when her husband had yelled at their five-year-old son, calling him "stupid" for something he had done. The little boy, looking shocked and puzzled, replied to his father, "Daddy, I know what I *did* was dumb, but *I* am not stupid!" Happily, in this case, his father saw the validity of his son's words and apologized to him. Children without healthy self-esteem, who have not learned this distinction in their own experience, lack the confidence to speak to an adult in this way.

Dear friends of ours adopted from a war-torn country a child who had been emotionally abandoned through the first year of her life. Her over-whelmed caretakers at the crowded orphanage had stuck a bottle in her mouth and had changed her diapers, but there had been no time for cuddling or comfort. Despite an outpouring of love and care from her adoptive parents, this child's impoverished sense of self resulted in years of aggressive behavior, social isolation, and the cultivation of a material-centered life to compensate for the emptiness she felt within. Children who are abandoned or abused, physically or emotionally, have a hard time embracing a positive sense of identity. Their feelings of shame translate into thoughts such as, "I don't count"; "I'm not worth caring about"; "I'll never amount to anything." When children lose heart at an early age, they are likely to suffer lingering consequences throughout their adult life.

Early childhood experiences are not the only way we lose heart. Some people suffer a string of losses and calamities in their adult lives that leave them reeling. It is hard to comprehend why certain persons suffer many more afflictions than others, as if they literally attract negative circumstances into their lives. It may be possible to trace their woes to unconscious self-negation, but that effort lies beyond our task. We only need to be aware that a person who has suffered repeated blows in adult life—physically, financially, or emotionally—will often sink into deep shame and depression.

People with a weak sense of self are among the most challenging for those of us in healing and helping professions. Even with years of therapy, it can be difficult to make up for the emotional losses of early childhood, and we cannot undo patterns of adult tragedy and pain.

Of course, we do not need to suffer from deep-seated shame or self-hatred to feel the weight of discouragement in our lives. The ordinary ups and downs of life provide many ways to lose heart! Even the most self-confident among us knows the sting of failure at times. At various periods of my ministry, I recall situations like these:

- Watching her marriage fall apart, a perfectly capable, gifted woman sinks into

5

feelings of guilt and despair, wondering if she is fit to live a married life at all.

- A child with wonderful imagination and mild dyslexia is held back in school for a year to gain reading skills, and feels deeply embarrassed; he sees all his friends go on to the next grade, and thinks he must be a dumb loser.

- A brilliant young professor makes a needlessly insensitive remark to a student and comes to see that his emotional and social skills have not caught up with his intellectual powers.

- A woman completely at ease and competent in her own cultural setting suffers a collapse of confidence as she tries to make her way in an unfamiliar culture.

Discouragement like this is generally circumstantial rather than deep-seated. Each of us has limitations and inadequacies that can result in a poor self-image under certain circumstances.

As spiritual caregivers, the first thing to understand is that we are not here to fix or solve one another's problems. We do not need to find solutions, achieve healing, or fill another person's emotional needs. Indeed, we cannot do these things, much as we might like to. The compassionate heart in us wants to rescue others from their pain. Yet the sooner we let go of the illusion that we can fix people's brokenness or heal their pain, the more helpful we are likely to be to them. We are not here to save others, but to point to a deeper source of healing and grace.

Practical Helps for Encouraging Healthy Self-Love

What can we offer to people whose sense of self has been wounded and diminished? What perspectives and practices of faith can help strengthen, reframe, or open possibilities of healing to someone whose capacity for authentic self-love has been shaken, frayed, or damaged?

1. *We can be present with our full attention and listen with active care.* This is one of the best ways to encourage others in their confused and disheartened state. To be fully present, without a sense of hurry, is in itself a witness to the value of the person you are with. It says, "You count; you are worth my time and care." This unspoken message serves as a counterweight to the internal messages of self-denigration playing in the head of someone struggling with self-worth. When we listen deeply and attentively to anyone, we are saying in effect, "What you think and feel and experience are important to me." Being taken seriously and listened to are among the most healing realities

we can offer individuals searching for a sense of their own value or seeking to reorient their lives following disorientation.

When we truly listen to a person, we discover that beyond spoken words we can "hear" emotions, gestures, physical postures, and facial expressions. We learn to "read" a more complete communication of feelings, to perceive the impact of a person's experience as well as the facts of a person's life. Beginning to understand a fellow human being this way is a genuine expression of Christian love—indeed one of its most important expressions. Listening well requires of us a certain maturity of spirit, a willingness to step out of ourselves and enter the reality and suffering of another's world. It asks of us a suspension of judgment, a welcoming patience that invites the speaker to discover what is within and find words to articulate his or her inner truth. Quaker teacher and author Douglas Steere highly valued this ministry of deep listening: "To 'listen' another's soul into a condition of disclosure and discovery may be almost the greatest service that any human being ever performs for another."[2]

Such listening becomes "holy listening" as we recognize God, present within and between us, in our speaking and listening. By grace, there are moments when the human listener drops away and the speaker encounters the Great Listener, who loves us without conditions and before whom our rationalizations are exposed, our motives purified, our prayers reordered. Then we begin to see both our true condition and our next step of the journey more clearly. Such is the gift we can offer one another through deep listening.

2. *We can offer messages of hope from our faith.* Perhaps the best place to begin is with the assurance of God's tremendous love. If you don't already do so, you might wish to start jotting down Bible passages that speak of divine love to human hearts, perhaps as you come upon them in your own devotional time. All of us need reassurance of a love far beyond our own capacity. Indeed, since human love can be both fragile and fickle, the idea of God's unconditional love can be hard to trust, especially when life circumstances seem to contradict it.

Here is where the promises of our faith become a beacon of hope, a bulwark against our natural doubts and fears. At times of turbulence and uncertainty in our lives, we frequently cling to the Scripture stories, teachings, and promises that most assure us. The following represent a few of the passages I return to often when seeking or sharing the certainty of divine love:

The Lord is compassionate
    and merciful,
        very patient, and full of faithful love.

. . . .

The Lord's faithful love is from
    forever ago to forever from now
        for those who honor him. (Ps. 103:8, 17)

When Israel was a child, I loved him,...
    I took them up in my arms,
    but they did not know
        that I healed them.
I led them
    with bands of human kindness,
    with cords of love.
I treated them like those
    who lift infants to their cheeks;
        I bent down to them and fed them. (Hos. 11:1-4)

God so loved the world that he gave his only Son, so
that everyone who believes in him won't perish but
will have eternal life. (John 3:16)

I am the good shepherd. The good shepherd lays
down his life for the sheep....No one has greater
love than to give up one's life for one's friends. (John
10:11; 15:13)

Who will separate us from Christ's love? Will we be
separated by trouble, or distress, or harassment,...or
danger, or sword?...I'm convinced that nothing can
separate us from God's love in Christ Jesus our Lord:

not death or life, not angels or rulers, not present
things or future things, not powers or height or depth,
or any other thing that is created. (Rom. 8:35, 38-39)

Those who dwell in self-denigration will often affirm God's love as a general principle but
struggle to believe that it applies to them personally. If this seems to be the case for any persons
you are visiting, you may assure them of this:
the witness of Jesus shows that God does indeed
love them personally, regardless of who they are
or what they have done or not done. In Christ,
God reveals a profound understanding of human
weakness and limitation, showing a far greater
willingness to forgive than we often have readi-
ness to receive. Indeed, the only thing that can
separate us from God's love in Christ is our own
unwillingness to receive the gift! Sometimes in
imagined unworthiness a person thinks, *God
wouldn't forgive someone as sinful or as stubborn as
me*, or *How could God possibly love someone as foolish as I have been?* But this seeming humility is really an odd form of arrogance. To make oneself a
permanent exception to God's grace is disguised
pride. Such self-deception is perhaps best pointed
out with humor and a gentle smile: "My! You
mean you're such a hopeless case, even God can't
love you?"

3. *We can remind believers of the wonderful gift of
their baptism.* In this sacrament, we are spiritually

united with Christ, joined with the mystical body of Christ. Thus we are promised that God sees us, in Christ, *as* the Beloved. The essence of the words God speaks to Jesus at *his* baptism—"You are my Son, the Beloved"—is also what the Spirit speaks to us through the faith community at *our* baptism: "You are my beloved child!" This promise is especially clear in the First Letter of John: "See what kind of love the Father has given to us in that we should be called God's children, and that is what we are!" (1 John 3:1). The assurance of our belovedness in baptism can be a deeply healing grace. The great reformer Martin Luther, when "beset with devils" and losing heart in his personal struggles, would touch his forehead and repeat aloud, "I am baptized; I am baptized!"

If those you are visiting have been baptized, you may find an appropriate moment to remind them of the meaning of their baptism and the assurance baptism gives us of being deeply loved by God. It can be helpful, if possible, to offer a simple ritual of baptismal remembrance. Ask those you are caring for if they would be willing to receive a physical reminder through water and touch. If so, get a cup of water, dip your fingers in, and touch the person's forehead with a few simple words, such as: "(Name), remember your baptism. Like Jesus, and with Jesus, you too are God's beloved!" You do not need to be ordained to offer the simple service of such a ritual. This is not the sacrament itself, but a sacramental act of remembrance.

4. *We can suggest a few spiritual practices that might be helpful to someone trying to discover or recover healthy self-esteem.* Only by God's grace does real healing of self-worth take place, yet certain practices can help set the stage for grace to operate more freely. Your suggestions may help a person find an interior opening of mind and heart to the deeper healing of the Spirit.

People who struggle to acknowledge their worth harbor an anxious sense of self. A helpful practice for those who fear they are not good enough to "deserve" God's love is the practice of simple faith affirmations. These are usually drawn directly from Scripture or from worship liturgies grounded in Scripture. They can be paraphrased or personalized so that the words apply directly to the one who speaks them. Here are a few examples based on the Scripture texts shared and the reminder of our baptismal identity:

- The Lord is compassionate, and full of faithful love for me.
- Nothing can separate me from God's love in Jesus Christ!
- Jesus, my good shepherd, loves me as a friend.
- I am baptized and beloved in Christ.

You can suggest such examples, but it may be more useful to help persons find their own affirmation. Ask, "What would you most like to believe and trust more deeply right now?" Work with them to clarify and simplify the statement they respond most strongly to and seem ready to claim for themselves. Explain that such affirmations may be spoken aloud or silently within one's heart. Generally one repeats the phrase inwardly for a few minutes, gently and slowly so as to savor the words and absorb their meaning. This is done several times a day, especially when anxious. It is a practice that helps calm distracting thoughts and feelings by focusing one's attention on God's loving presence. You might suggest that people write down their affirmation on a sticky note or small card, placing it where it will regularly catch their attention—perhaps on a laptop rim, bathroom mirror, or bedside table. Some people create a banner for their computer screen from such an affirmation, where it greets them before they begin desk work.

Another wonderful practice for healing the wounded self is what seasoned pastor and author Flora Wuellner calls "Soaking Prayer," and what I have often taught as "Prayer of Presence."[3] It involves imagining ourselves in a safe and beautiful place where we can relax, perhaps stretch out physically, and simply allow ourselves to absorb the gift of God's love. God's love might be imagined as bright sunlight gently enveloping us, softly radiating around and through us. Or it might be imagined as an ocean of love on which we float in deep trust, buoyed by grace. As our imagination opens us to a helpful image, we may find a deep sense of healing, assurance, peace, and comfort. The essential practice is simply to remain quietly in God's loving presence, without effort or tension. It is an experience of allowing God to be God while we soak up gifts of divine love and healing grace, letting them penetrate our hidden depths. Open receptivity is the key.

As someone offering spiritual care, you can invite persons into this form of prayer while you are with them, leading it with simple words of guidance. You might prefer to copy or describe it, inviting them to try it out in their own way and at their own pace.

When we encourage others to trust their belovedness in God's heart, and teach simple practices for receiving and absorbing divine love, we help others open to the Spirit's work of healing deep wounds. People may not even know or remember these wounds from their childhood. The Spirit can work without our conscious knowledge and can bring things back to memory if needed or helpful. As trust in God's love for them grows, people who had no confidence that they were worthy of such love begin to develop their God-given capacity for healthy self-esteem. To know ourselves loved and our worth affirmed by God—this is surely one of the most important forms of encouragement we can ever help others reach for, or receive for ourselves.

Prayer

God of infinite love and embracing mercy,

Look with tender understanding on your beloved child, (name),

> who yearns for deep acceptance and the assurance of your love,
>
> yet fears (she or he) may not be worthy of such blessing.

Help (name) remember the gift of (his or her) baptism,

> to know in the depths of (his or her) heart the truth of your accepting grace by virtue of fellowship with Jesus, your beloved Son.

Enfold (name) with the assurance of (his or her) own belovedness as your (daughter or son).

May the love of Christ give (her or him) courage;

> may the grace of your Holy Spirit fill (her or him);
>
> may your fatherly gentleness and mothering strength embrace and heal
>> all that would prevent (name) from accepting and respecting (himself or herself):

deep-rooted shame; painful rejection; embarrassment;
loss of confidence in (his or her) value, goodness, or gifts.

By your grace, restore (name's) hope for a more healed and whole future,
and (his or her) trust in your goodness and love for each step of the journey ahead.

We ask this in the name and spirit of Christ, our great assurance. Amen.

Further Scriptures on God's Love

Psalms 89:1-2; 108:4; 118:1-4; 1 John 4:9, 16, 19; all the stories of Jesus' healings; raising the son of the widow of Nain.

Related Quotations

Every person matters to God. No one gets lost in the crowd. Each one is unique, precious, beloved....God's loving power longs to enfold and flood through all that we are—our subconscious as well as conscious selves; our wounded memories; our damaged trust; our fears; our shadow sides; our hidden hopes; the deep gifts within us not yet born or long forgotten; our attitudes toward ourselves, others, the world around us, and God....As we are healed, made whole, and filled with God, we become more our unique selves, not less....We are each individually handcrafted. (Flora Slosson Wuellner, *Miracle: When Christ Touches Our Deepest Need* [Nashville: Upper Room Books, 2008], 14–16)

Each of us has an inner Bartimaeus crying out, often unheard or ignored by those around us and sometimes even by ourselves....What we call our negative sides—anger, anxiety, complaining, criticizing, procrastinating, controlling—are usually deep inner cries for help. Perhaps they are cries from early childhood, rising from emotional wounds that never healed. We were told so often to get over them, rise above them, forgive and forget, concentrate on the positive, that we thrust down these unhealed wounds below our conscious level.

But wounds do not just go away. If unhealed, they cry like abandoned children in the dark, forgotten places within us. The only way they can make their presence felt is through our negative attitudes, our addictive escapes, all symptoms of pain. (Wuellner, *Miracle*, 25)

CHAPTER 2

The Courage to Work from One's Center

It is not difficult to see intrinsic connections between our relationship to self and our relationship with work. The human sense of self is deeply formed and influenced by the realm of labor. When we can rise to the challenges of good work, we feel effective and courageous; we see ourselves growing and learning, becoming competent and creative in our tasks. The satisfaction of making something well, discovering a fresh vision, creating new resources, achieving solutions to difficult problems, or affecting people's lives in positive ways—all feed into healthy self-esteem and sense of purpose.

Conversely, we become demoralized and diminished in our sense of self when we feel we are not contributing anything of real value to

others, our work setting is chronically dysfunc-
tional, or the unspoken culture of the organization for which we work violates our ethics and
integrity. And if we cannot even find meaningful
work, or good work has been taken from us by
job loss or forced retirement, discouragement can
set in with real force.

It seems that our culture's relationship to work
has undergone a substantial shift over the past
fifty years or so. This shift makes it harder to connect who we are with what we do, or, put another
way, to keep soul and role connected.[1] Here are
a few trends I have observed as part of the shift:

- Opportunities to find meaningful work
  appropriate to our level of education can
  no longer be assumed. It used to be that
  those who graduated from high school
  could be reasonably assured of finding a
  job suited to their level of education, often
  within or near the place they were raised.
  It was also generally true that those with a
  college degree could be assured of higher
  wage earnings and interesting job options,
  especially if they were willing to relocate
  periodically. With farming taken over by
  huge agribusinesses, manufacturing jobs
  shipped overseas, and technology assum-
  ing more importance than liberal arts edu-

cation, these connections no longer hold true in the same way.

- Employment with a large company or firm used to offer job security and benefits for the long haul. When my father's cousin joined a certain large, well-established business firm, he could count on a business culture that provided ways to move up the company ladder, held out the promise of increasing wages and benefits, and elicited a strong bond of company loyalty. By the time my brother joined the same firm, its culture was shifting. Thirty years later, with fewer opportunities for upward mobility in the organization, virtually no job security, and many workers forced to set up home offices at their own expense, there has been substantial loss of trust in—or loyalty to—the company. It is hard for workers to feel enthusiastic or deeply committed to the success of any corporation that appears to value shareholders far above employees. Why should one give heart and soul to an employer with neither?

- Fifty years ago, thanks to the hard-earned rights of labor unions, most workers enjoyed limited work hours. They could count on regular leisure with family as well as time to develop hobbies, offer volunteer services, or engage in local civic duties. But in a globally competitive economy, the trend among corporations, businesses, and factories is toward fewer workers, each with a substantially greater workload and far less time to nurture their personal lives or contribute to their communities. The very concept of Sabbath has been largely lost in our culture, and most large-scale enterprises now operate on a 24/7 basis.

As a result of changes like these, many people in our time feel disconnected from, dissatisfied by, or disgruntled with their work. Some feel stuck in jobs that hold no interest for them, and lose motivation to do things well. Others find that their work, while good in itself, does not fit their gifts or skills. A job that does not correspond well with a person's sense of self will not prove fulfilling or meaningful. In some cases, the nature of the work is directly opposed to a person's deeper values and beliefs. Yet under the constraints of financial necessity, or perhaps the conflicting needs of a spouse and children, people may feel obliged to stick with a job that clearly lacks integrity for them. Their work creates a painful interior state of division and conflict. Either "soul" and "role" part company and live in separate mental quarters, or they become warring factions within. People are left with no clear sense of a greater purpose or call in the work they do.

In other situations, the work may be right and a sense of vocation strong but job pressures are inhumane. I imagine you know, as I do, colleagues, friends, and family members who are deeply committed to their professions and overwhelmed by their workload. Most of them feel compelled—either by external or internal demands—to maintain punishing work schedules just to get the job done. When I suggest to a person the value of setting reasonable boundaries on work hours, I am often met with one of two responses: expressed fear of losing a job to someone superiors perceive as a more dedicated worker, or an image of self driven by the need to excel in every detail so that "enough" is never enough. The two responses are not unrelated; perfectionist self-expectations are often rooted in fears of being considered insufficient. Since most of us harbor at least some measure of insecurity regarding our work competency, it is small wonder that so many of us suffer from profound anxiety, exhaustion, and discouragement about work in relation to the rest of our lives.

Moreover, in an economic recession such as we have recently been experiencing, occasions for feeling discouraged are multiplied. The loss of a job, especially over a long period, can be financially disastrous. It can also be emotionally painful, involving erosion of self-respect, diminished autonomy and choice, and the loss of a work community where important relationships have formed over time. Culturally we do not tend to see the loss of a job as an occasion of grief, but surely it is so for many. One helpful thing we can do with persons who have suffered job loss is invite them to recognize and name the various dimensions of loss they have experienced along with their job. The stages of grief that apply to losing an important personal relationship through divorce or death can also apply to losing meaningful work. Denial, anger, bargaining, depression, and eventual acceptance may all need to be worked through. It can be helpful—even eye-opening for some—simply to point this out.

Trying persistently but unsuccessfully to find a job easily undermines our sense of capability and value to the larger human community. Although difficult at any age, it can be especially disorienting for young adults, who are normally setting their course of independence and gaining experience in a new career at this stage of their lives. An unusually high percentage of young adults these days are finding themselves with no viable financial option but to move back in with their parents. This can lead to a deep sense of frustration about delayed dreams, including the postponement of major decisions involving marriage and family life. The longer situations like this continue, the more likely people are to despair of finding the freedom and growth they long to discover and express through meaningful work.

At the other end of the life spectrum lies the experience of retirement. For some, retirement is an immense relief, a long-anticipated emancipation from the constraints and frustrations of work. For others it feels premature, unwelcomed, or unnatural; the perceived end of a productive career may arrive with the smell of death. Men often feel this more keenly than women, since culturally speaking men have tended to find their primary sense of identity through work, whereas women have generally found their deeper sense of identity through relationships. Yet both men and women who have spent decades in the work force may suffer in retirement from feelings of emptiness or loss of meaning. Without a role that gives concrete definition and shape to their days, they often wonder who they are. Especially for those who have had little time to develop interests, hobbies, or relationships outside of work, retirement can pose substantial challenges.

Whether it comes through loss of confidence in one's work abilities, loss of vocational meaning and purpose, loss of hope for a better future, or just feeling stuck in an impossible job, when the sense of identity or meaning derived from one's work disappears, it can lead to serious anxiety or depression. These, in turn, easily lead to self-destructive choices such as depending on drugs or alcohol to dull emotional pain, or filling an emotional vacuum with compulsive sex or gambling.

If you sense that a person you are visiting or working with is seriously depressed, or learn that he or she is engaged in addictive behaviors, you will want to refer him or her to professionals who understand the medical aspects of these problems and how to treat them. Make a list of hotline numbers and contact information for a few trusted mental health professionals. Keep it easily accessible so you can make appropriate referrals to any you may encounter whose physical and emotional well-being seems truly to be in danger.

The Limitations of Advice Giving

For most people you are likely to visit, encouragement is good medicine. Please be aware that encouragement and advice are minimally overlapping circles, even if many of us tend to confuse the two. We often assume that our well-intentioned advice, or hard-won pearls of life wisdom, will naturally be an encouragement to others. This is not the case as often as we might think.

Some of our ordinary ways of trying to encourage people are not especially effective and may even elicit the opposite of what we intend. For example, despite their widespread use, it is rare that cheerful platitudes are comforting: "God is probably testing your faith; you just need to be patient and persevere." "Why don't you get out and soak up some sunshine? I'm sure that will brighten your outlook!" "Put it all in Jesus' hands, and he'll help you sort it out."

If you are tempted to reach into a proverbial "bag of bromides," ask yourself whether you really believe what you are saying and why you think it would help someone else. Most of us have resorted to simplistic conventions like this at one time or another. We tend to turn to the trite when we don't really know what to say or are uncomfortable sitting quietly with a person absorbed in pain and uncertainty.

As you sit with someone enduring a real struggle, become aware of how you yourself are feeling. Are you anxious? Do you feel a driving need to rescue the other person from his or her dilemma? Are you afraid you will seem incompetent or feel useless if you cannot help the other person find a solution to his or her problem? Are you comfortable being together in silence when words seem to cease being helpful?

The more anxious we feel, the more likely we are to resort—overtly or covertly—to advice

27

giving. We dwell in a culture of fixers, savers, and advice givers. Many of us imagine that operating this way is one of the most helpful things we can do for others. Perhaps for very practical and mundane concerns this is true. But in matters pertaining to heart and soul, even our very best advice for fixing or solving a problem is unlikely to be of genuine or lasting help to another. Where internal values and decisions are concerned, people need to go into their depths to find the answers held within their own souls. They need to listen to the indwelling Spirit, access their inner wisdom, and discover their own deepest truth, which at root connects with divine realities.

Remember, *encouragement* means helping another person recover her or his own heart. And the biblical meaning of *heart* is not mere emotion, but rather the center of one's whole inner being: reason, feeling, intuition, and will joined in the unique shape of a person's defining character. Henri Nouwen speaks to this in *Bread for the Journey*: "The word courage comes from the Latin word *cor*, which means 'heart.'...The heart is the center...of all our thoughts, feelings, passions, and decisions....A courageous life, therefore, is a life lived from the center....'Have courage' therefore means 'Let your center speak.'"[2] Encouragement involves us in helping others locate their own center and begin to live from its depths as their primary source of energy and direction.

Having said this, there are times when a person will *directly ask* for advice or counsel. There is a role for constructive suggestions and the offering of basic resources. In such cases, a few guidelines may help prevent you from falling into the trap of trying to fix or solve another person's problem.

1. Pay attention to your use of language. Avoid imperatives and adopt invitations. Instead of saying, "You *should* learn about..." "You *ought* to try..." or, "You *must* believe..." turn to invitational phrases like, "It seems to me that..." "It could be useful to..." or, "You might wish to consider..." Offer your thoughts as possibilities, not presumed solutions. Questions can be a helpful way to gently introduce counsel: "Have you thought about this option?" or, "Are you aware of this resource?"

2. In limited circumstances it can be useful to draw explicitly on aspects of your own experience. I suggest you do so only if your sharing meets these criteria:

   a. You do so infrequently and very judiciously, with strong reason to think your similar experience may be useful to someone else.

   b. You recognize and indicate clearly that your experience may not fit the other's need.

   c. You do not press what you learned from your experience on the other.

   d. You offer it with complete freedom to be received or laid aside as the other sees fit.

Let your learning simply widen the pool of options, trusting it to spark insight and connections in the person you are with. If a person is *not* asking for advice, it is best to refrain from suggestions in any form, no matter how invitational.

Learning to Ask Open, Honest Questions

If giving advice is of limited value, what are some practices we can embody as spiritual caregivers to encourage others in the relationship of self and work, soul and role? Instead of offering resources, solutions, or insights from your own experience, try learning the art of open, honest questions.[3] An *honest* question is one you do not know the answer to. It cannot be advice disguised in question form, as are some of the questions suggested above. An *open* question offers room for others to explore their inner terrain, rather than closing down possibilities: "How are you feeling about this?" is an open question; "Why do you seem irritated?" is not. When you try to name what another person is feeling based on vocal inflection, facial expression, or body posture, you are engaged in interpretation. The purpose of open, honest questions is to help others name and interpret their own thoughts and feelings.

Such questions are not driven by curiosity or a problem-solving agenda on your part. Their sole purpose is to allow others to engage their own discernment process more fully.

For you to be truly at ease with the value of open, honest questions, you will need to cultivate your trust that each person you encounter has his or her own inner wisdom. Our Christian tradition calls this wisdom "the indwelling Christ." Jesus says, "Remain in me, and *I will remain in you....* I am the vine; you are the branches" (John 15:4-5, emphasis added). Paul writes to the Colossians of the great mystery "which is *Christ living in you*, the hope of glory" (Col. 1:27, emphasis added). We also use the language of the *indwelling Spirit*: "Don't you know that your body is a temple of *the Holy Spirit who is in you?*" (1 Cor. 6:19, emphasis added). As Christians we affirm that wisdom—however obscured by our brokenness—dwells in *all* persons by virtue of the image of God in which all are made. Quakers call this wisdom the "Inner Light" or "Inner Teacher."

If you learn to trust the reality of inner wisdom in others, you will find that people access it best when their souls are free, invited, and supported without judgment. Parker Palmer notes that when our souls feel demanded or coerced, they go into hiding.[4] Sadly, the church has a history of trying to coerce people into belief through fear and judgment, sending countless souls into hiding. A constructed "religious self" then takes the place of an alive, creative, and inquiring soul.

When you visit persons struggling to discern their path or vocation in life, you have an opportunity to trust the divine image within them, however deeply buried it may be. This confidence can be a great help when you are offering spiritual support to people who have fallen away from the institutional church, or who struggle with matters of faith and doubt. They, too, have within their souls "that of God in every person," a deep source of wisdom and inner knowing.

When you sit with people discouraged by vocational confusion, or who seek clarity about their direction in life, help them explore their own inner wisdom with questions like these:

- What activities or interests in your life bring you the greatest joy or energy?

- What kind of activity or focus leaves you drained, bored, or restless?

- When have you felt most alive in your work?

- What would you dream about doing if there were no financial or relational constraints on your choices?

- Where do you feel a sense of rightness about the work you do (or want to do)?

- What use of your gifts and abilities gives

you the greatest sense of satisfaction or feeling of significance?

- What kind of work gives you hope for the future?
- Where does the deeper call in your life seem to be surfacing?
- How would you need to rearrange your life to make a new choice possible?

Some people you encounter may have a strong, clear sense of their true vocation yet suffer exhaustion from the pace and intensity of this very work. In these cases, you will need to shift gears, suiting your questions and suggested spiritual practices to their reality. Christians and Jews share the heritage of a Sabbath command, yet our culture no longer supports Sabbath time as a necessary value. Consequently, work pressures easily spill into evenings, weekends, holidays, and even vacation time for many people. How can we encourage overly dedicated workers to care for their own bodies and souls in this 24/7 world?

Practices to Encourage Sabbath Time

- Have a conversation with the persons concerned about the importance of Sabbath time in human life. How do they understand the value of Sabbath? When and where do they experience the qualities of time unpressured by the need to achieve or produce? What benefits, physical or spiritual, do they receive from such time?

- Share a few of the reflections on Sabbath found at the end of this chapter, or add related quotations you find meaningful. Offer them as messages of encouragement to build "breathing room" into our lives. Since most Christians need to take the practice of Sabbath more to heart in overly busy schedules, feel free to share honest struggles of your own in this regard (without allowing the focus to move too much to you).

- Invite the person you are with to reflect on a few of the following questions:

  ○ When or where do you feel most at peace?

  ○ When or where do you feel closest to God?

  ○ What do your responses suggest about the kind of Sabbath time you need?

  ○ What prevents you from taking this time?

- Suggest taking a "Sabbath walk," which Wayne Muller describes as time to "let your soul catch up with you."[5] This is a half-hour walk, preferably in the natural world, where you don't aim to get anywhere. Instead, you allow your senses to draw you to whatever you notice, taking your leisure to observe, touch, smell, and explore things that catch your attention. "Follow your own timing and curiosity," counsels Muller. After thirty minutes, notice what has happened inside you.

- If people feel it is impossible to build a regular day or even half day of true Sabbath into their lives, ask how they might creatively "salt their days" with Sabbath moments. What might those moments look and feel like for them?

- Ask those you are with how it feels to say no to something—an invitation, a demand, even perhaps a good opportunity. Wonder together why saying no is so hard in our culture. Share thoughts on how setting boundaries is life-giving!

- If it fits your conversation, you might describe a few principles of discernment that can help us decide what to say yes or no to.

  ○ There is a difference between our gifts and our skills. When we are operating out of our deepest, truest gifts, our work feeds and energizes us. When we are operating primarily out of learned skills, we will eventually wear out, even if the work is successful and we are receiving praise for it.

○ The fact that a need exists, and we have skills to answer that need, does not necessarily mean we should respond to it. The timing may not be right for us, or it may be a true soul-task for someone else with similar skills. The deeper question to attend to is: Will this choice be life giving for me as well as for others at this time?

• If a person seems unclear about what his or her deeper gifts really are, you can suggest that a spiritual gifts inventory might be useful.[6] Discovering what our best gifts are, particularly when those who know us well affirm them, can be an immense gift of encouragement!

Although the spiritual practices suggested here are directed primarily toward issues involving the relationship of soul and role, they can also be deeply helpful in our relationships with self, others, and God. Refraining from advice-giving is certainly a good rule of thumb in all our relations with others, and the art of asking open, honest questions can be just as helpful in relations with family, friends, and colleagues as in relation to our work or vocation. Sabbath time allows the very space we need to deepen our relationship with God and grow in a healthy relationship to our authentic self. You will undoubtedly find many ways to connect these suggested practices to all aspects of human relatedness.

Below you will find a prayer, further Scripture texts, and quotations from various spiritual writers pertaining to the themes of this chapter. I hope a few may be of help to people you visit and support.

Prayer

God of Life,

Your creativity is expressed in all that we know, and your creation is ongoing through all time. We praise you for making us in your own image, with gifts of creativity, skill, and insight to offer others. We thank you for making us capable of becoming cocreative with you in bringing goodness, healing, and meaning into this world through our work.

Be near to (name), who is feeling discouraged in relation to (his or her) work. Confirm to (him or her) the true nature of (his or her) gifts and abilities. Help (him or her) see more clearly how to use these gifts for the benefit of others. Open to (him or her) the way forward into a greater sense of satisfaction in new learning, labor well done, contributions made to a larger whole, and a deeper sense of purpose in (his or her) life. May the right opportunities come (name's) way according to your good intentions for (him or her).

Lift (name's) heavy heart, renew (his or her) courage, refresh (his or her) spirit—all for the sake of your great love and good purpose. In Christ's name we pray, Amen.

Related Texts and Quotations

I know the plans I have in mind for you, declares the Lord; they are plans for peace, not disaster, to give you a future filled with hope. (Jer. 29:11)

Do not neglect the gift that is in you. (1 Tim. 4:14 NRSV)

Everyone has the right, perhaps even the imperative, to reach for self-expression not to gratify every whim but to serve as one was created to serve....Only when we act expressively do we move toward full aliveness and authentic power....An expressive act is one taken because if I did not take it I would be denying my own insight, gift, nature. (Parker J. Palmer, *The Active Life* [San Francisco: Jossey-Bass, 1990], 20, 24)

If we are not true to the new life that is rising within us—if we deny, repress, or live in contradiction to it—we invite internal havoc and trigger war within ourselves. (Suzanne G. Farnham et al., *Listening Hearts: Discerning God's Call in Community* [Harrisburg, PA: Morehouse Publishing, 1991], 24)

To be doing what is good can be the greatest obstacle to doing something even better. (Farnham et al., *Listening Hearts*, 26)

Our lack of rest and reflection is not just a personal affliction. It colors the way we build and sustain community, it dictates the way we respond to suffering, and it shapes the ways in which we seek peace and healing in the world. (Wayne Muller, *Sabbath: Restoring the Sacred Rhythm of Rest* [New York: Bantam Books, 1999], 3)

There is a pervasive form of contemporary violence...activism and overwork....To surrender to too many demands, to commit oneself to too many projects...destroys the fruitfulness of our own work, because it kills the root of inner wisdom which makes work fruitful. (Abridged from Thomas Merton, *Conjectures of a Guilty Bystander* [Garden City, NY: Doubleday, 1966], 81)

It is not possible to help everybody. Being endlessly available to anyone or everyone is good for no one. (Ester de Waal, *Seeking God: The Way of St. Benedict* [Collegeville, MN: Liturgical Press, 1984], 138)

If God sets apart one day to rest, we can too. There are some things that can be accomplished, even by God, only in a state of rest....The precedent to quit doing and simply *be* is divine. (Eugene Peterson, "Rhythms of Grace," *Weavings* viii, no. 2 (1993): 17)

CHAPTER 3

The Courage to Grow
in Relationships

Many of our great discouragements grow out of relational difficulties. It is almost impossible to separate our personal sense of identity from primary relationships in our lives. Earlier we noted how early relationships in family and school can shape our sense of who we are in harmful or positive ways. The connection between sense of self and relationship with others is paradoxical: on the one hand, we must finally claim who we are in our deepest self without allowing others to define us. On the other hand, we cannot become fully human in solitary splendor, but only through relationships of mutual care and supportive if challenging love. Our very humanity depends on the quality and character of our relationships with God, self, others, and the wider world—

including whole communities of creatures and the ecologies within which we coexist on earth.

The capacity for healthy and fruitful relationships is one of our greatest human potentials in God's splendid design for "life in all its fullness." Yet living out this potential remains the most elusive of all human goals. Our relationships form the daily crucible in which self-interest and other-centered love compete for our attention and energy. Those who live in families probably know this crucible best within home life, while those who live alone may experience it more at work or in a faith community.

Relationships in the Bible and the Call of Love

The Bible is full of stories about human relationships in all their complexity. With undisguised and sometimes uncomfortable candor, Scripture shows us a full array of broken, tangled, crafty, and violent relationships alongside faithful, patient, courageous, and healing relationships. In the very first chapter of Genesis, following Adam and Eve's fall from intimacy with God, we are confronted with bloodshed between their two sons, Cain and Abel. In a stunningly rapid deterioration from Eden's exile to fratricide, this ancient tale reminds us that when our relationship with God is out of kilter, the consequences in human life are immediate and devastating.

The Bible does not shield us from stories of rape and incest, jealousy and revenge, deceit and treachery. It does not soften the story of King David's lust, adultery, and murder. The prophets mince no words describing the sins of Israel, and are quick to link the nation's faithlessness to God with their mistreatment of one another. When it comes to Jesus' life, the Bible continues to portray every kind of human failing—from the crowds, religious leaders, political figures, and even Jesus' disciples. Moreover, the Gospels and the Epistles are written in a way that does not permit us to exempt ourselves. They compel us to recognize the failings of our own lives so as to confess them.

Whatever a person's relational struggles, a Scripture story can likely be found to mirror its basic dynamics, which have not changed much in the intervening millennia! Thankfully, Scripture is also full of guidance for learning how to relate to one another from a mind-set different from the one that gets us in trouble. The troublemaking mind-set is rooted in self-interest, ignorance, and inattention, along with the accepted assumptions and conventions of culture. Scripture consistently counsels us to keep God at the center rather than self or culture. It teaches knowledge of both the human and the divine heart, and tirelessly calls us back to sacred attentiveness.

How do we learn to turn away from self-interest and conventional assumptions as the unconscious governing principles of our lives? It seems to me that Scripture suggests three primary paths:

1. *Worship*. When we worship God in spirit and truth, we find adoration and praise at the center of our heart. Praise tends to take us out of ourselves, and our ordinary frame of reference, to a focus on divine worthiness. Humble adoration carries us into deep delight at the wonder, goodness, creative power, and love of God.

2. *Prayer*. Prayer gathers up every aspect of human life and spiritual reality, from silently contemplating divine Presence to entering the heart of Christ in intercession for others. Both contemplative and intercessory forms of prayer carry us out of self-absorption; contemplative prayer is more effective in breaking through our cultural conditioning.

3. *Service*. Serving others opens us to the world and its tremendous needs. We often discover in service a great sense of happiness, meaning, and purpose. Through it we come to recognize our common humanity with those we might never imagine having much in common with. Service is effective in moving us out of self-absorption and in giving us broader perspective on our cultural assumptions. It tends to move us toward a deeper commitment to God's justice in the world.

Generous giving and active hospitality are further extensions of these three. Both help move us from a self-preoccupied to a God-directed life. All five are essentially ways of grounding ourselves in God's love and expressing it.

The deepest teachings of Scripture concern learning to love as God loves. Love is paradoxical, a truth expressed in the following couplet:

> You cannot give love if you don't have it.
> And you only have it if you give it.[1]

Our greatest challenge is to receive the love of God so deeply in our souls that it overflows us. By nature love outflows its boundaries, giving itself joyously like a spring that cannot cease bubbling upward. Love is perhaps the only reality in the cosmos that increases by expending itself. The flow of love is stimulated as we spend it on others.

Our Tangled Relationships

Our human relationships provide no end of occasions to learn how to love as God loves. If we began to see every hurt, frustration, disappointment, and irritation in our relationships as an opportunity to grow in love, the world would start to look different. But we are locked into narrow ways of seeing and relating to one another. In our families, we play certain roles that change complexion over time. Parenting a four-year-old and parenting a twenty-four-year-old are very different tasks. Relating to a parent as a teenager and relating to an elderly parent in midlife are quite different challenges. If we are growing in marriage, we will not relate to our spouse the same way we did on our honeymoon. Yet many of our expressions of relationship get stuck in old roles and old wounds. We develop ideas about one another based on certain experiences, which harden into judgments and reactions that continue shaping our relationships for decades, even generations.

A child grows up with an emotionally distant father, and develops a habit of indifference to everything his father does. This is the son's emotional defense—pretending he doesn't care about his dad since his dad never seemed to care much about him. Beneath the indifference lies a hidden ache for a real connection with his father, but the son cannot acknowledge this yearning, even to himself. After a midlife crisis, his father begins to recognize the pattern of his distance and what lies behind it. He tries to reach out to his son, awkwardly, since he has little practice. His son spurns him in subconscious revenge, lashing out in accumulated grief and anger for all the years of neglect. The father, hurt and not fully comprehending, withdraws.

A young couple, madly in love, get married. They do not know that each one is projecting onto the other an ideal image of how the other will meet her or his personal needs. Within a few years, it becomes apparent that the other is not living up to the projected ideal. Harping criticisms begin, then accusations: "You never..." "You always..." "Why don't you ever...?" The desire to change the other person takes center stage in the relationship, and a battle of wills ensues. Controlling advice abounds: "You should think about..." "You need to see..." "You must try to..." When these fail to achieve the desired end, threats are near at hand: "If you don't..., I will..."

A brother and sister grow up with a great deal of friction and fighting. The boy is clumsy and pugnacious, breaking toys unintentionally, talking loudly of things that irritate or embarrass his sister, and consistently denying responsibility for whatever harm he has caused. As he grows older and becomes more aggressive, she takes refuge in the world of her own friends, avoiding her brother as much as possible. By young adulthood, they are deeply estranged. They move to different parts of the country and know little about each other as the years pass, nor do they seem to care to know.

There are ten thousand variations of relational brokenness and alienation. The basic dynamics of difficult relationships are generally rooted in emotional immaturity. Each of us needs to grow emotionally, just as we grow physically or spiritually. Yet most of us receive little training on how to grow into more mature relationships, and so rely by default on our own family patterns, which may or may not be helpful. Physical or mental disabilities that occur as a result of birth, accident, illness, or aging can greatly complicate relational issues. Alcoholism, drug addiction, or sexual abuse—any of which may be the result of relational dysfunction—will in turn create even more confusing and chaotic relationships.

Family life is not the only arena in which we can become deeply discouraged about our relationships. Friendships may turn sour or evaporate. For some, an experience of betrayal by a very close friend can be as sharp a blow as infidelity in marriage. Estranged friendships are among the most difficult relationships to salvage, since they are often easier to avoid or escape when thing go bad.

What about relationships with colleagues, supervisors, church members, neighbors, acquaintances, and even strangers? Each offers opportunities for smooth sailing or shipwreck! We even have internalized relationships with people we know only by reputation or media exposure, such as famous musicians, actors, TV personalities, and politicians. We live in an era when many people, perhaps you and me included, feel deeply discouraged by our collective relationship with our elected leaders.

Spiritual Practices for Maturing in Relationship

We cannot bring others to maturity, but we can encourage them to recognize signs of their need to grow and offer a few paths into greater relational maturity. The Apostle Paul urges believers to grow up into Christ: "God's goal is for us to become mature adults—to be fully grown, measured by the standard of the fullness of Christ. As a result, we aren't supposed to be infants any longer who can be tossed and blown around by every wind.... Instead, by speaking the truth with love, let's grow in every way into Christ" (Eph. 4:13-15).

Growing up in every way includes emotional and spiritual growth, along with physical and mental development. Our culture places much greater emphasis on the physical and mental than on the emotional and spiritual. Humanity as a whole suffers from inadequate attention to both the emotional and spiritual realms. Thus we are preoccupied, personally and corporately, with security, order, control, pleasure, and absolutes.[2] We tend to like our religion and politics painted in black-and-white absolutes as well. Yet as long as we are arrested at a child's level of emotional maturity, we cannot discover the deeper spiritual truths God offers us.

As pastors, Stephen ministers, and others who offer spiritual care to people within the fold of the church, we do well to recognize our own need for continued growth alongside those we hope to help.

One of the tools you can familiarize yourself with, and introduce people to, is a guide to self-assessment in emotional health. The following summary lists stages of emotional maturity and the general characteristics of each stage.[3]

Emotional Health Self-Assessment

Emotional Infancy

- Want others to care for us and see others as objects to meet our needs
- Are driven by need for instant gratification
- Have difficulty entering another person's world

Emotional Childhood

- Are content when we get what we want; complain, withdraw, manipulate, seek

revenge, and get sarcastic when we don't get our way
- Are easily hurt, and take disagreement as a personal offense
- Unravel with stress, disappointment, or trials
- Have difficulty discussing our needs and wants clearly and calmly

Emotional Adolescence
- Are preoccupied with ourselves
- Are threatened by criticism and tend to be defensive
- Are critical and judgmental
- Have difficulty truly hearing another's pain, disappointment, or needs
- Deal poorly with conflict, often blaming, appeasing, or pouting; going to a third party; or ignoring the problem
- Keep tabs on what we give so we can later ask for something in return

Emotional Adulthood
- Ask clearly and honestly for what we need, want, or prefer
- Recognize, manage, and take responsibility for our own thoughts and feelings

- State our own beliefs and values without becoming adversarial

- Respect others without having to change them

- Give people room to make mistakes, not expecting perfection

- Appreciate persons for who they are, not for what they give back

- Accurately assess our own limits, strengths, and weaknesses, and freely discuss them with others

- Enter the feelings, needs, and concerns of others without losing ourselves

- Resolve conflict and negotiate solutions that take account of others' perspectives

As adults, most of us will find aspects of our emotional life described in more than one stage. We may see elements of our emotional childhood and adolescence predominating in our lives. Or we may see a mixture of adolescence and adulthood. This suggests, not surprisingly, that we are unevenly developed in our emotional lives. It takes practice to grow up emotionally, and we need support from others who are committed to maturing. Even more, we need modeling from elders, friends, or mentors who exhibit a greater degree of emotional maturity than we see in ourselves.

Feel free to copy this self-assessment, reproduced on pages 98–100 at the back of this book, and offer it as a resource for persons struggling with relational discouragement. It lists specific expressions of immaturity and maturity that most of us can recognize right away. Suggest that they use it as a tool for reflection and self-examination, asking themselves:

- In what ways do I express the characteristics of these stages?
- Which stages seem most dominant in my life?
- How do my less mature characteristics affect my important relationships?
- Do certain relationships in my life elicit one stage more than another? Why?
- What specific steps might I take to grow into greater emotional maturity?
- Who can best help me with this process?

In some instances, it might be helpful for a person to share this assessment with whomever they are having difficulty with. For example, a married couple might be able to use the list in a sequence like this: first, a time for separate personal self-examination; then a sharing of each person's self-assessment (*not* other-assessment!); followed by thoughts on how each would like to grow into greater self-awareness and more adult emotional responsibility. It is crucial that each person speaks only for himself or herself. The process might also work with parents and adult children, or between friends or coworkers, presuming both persons have enough maturity to reflect in this way.

When such work cannot be done between two people in conflict, this tool may still be helpful to persons you are visiting or counseling, if they seem willing and capable of honest self-reflection. You might invite them to work with the categories for a period of time so that they begin to see themselves more clearly as various characteristics get expressed in their daily relationships. Tracking in a journal what they notice in their feelings and behaviors can be very useful. At some point, they might want to list the characteristics of "Emotional Adulthood" on a card to tuck in a pocket or purse, post by their laptop, or bookmark their Bible. It would offer a simple way of reminding and encouraging themselves to keep growing in the attributes of a mature emotional life.

Simply naming these attributes can help some people begin to reframe their lives with a sense of hope about what is possible. Yet to grow into emotional adulthood at a practical level, we need to develop new habits of mind, heart, and tongue. Here are a few practices you can share that aid in developing greater emotional and spiritual maturity:

1. Learn to speak to others using "I" statements, speaking honestly only for yourself—your personal understandings, feelings, beliefs, values, hopes, and needs.

2. Learn to listen more truly and fully to others. This means being fully present, not interrupting, refraining from expressing strong reactions either vocally or with facial expressions, resisting the habit of formulating your own answer while the other is speaking, and allowing yourself to risk opening to the other's reality.

3. Learn to withhold judgment, especially condemnation. Others will not feel safe enough to become more truthful, vulnerable, and transparent when they feel condemned or dismissed; they will remain defended against the pain of rejection.

4. Learn to accept others as, and where, they are now. This involves acknowledging that differences of perspective, interpretation, behavior, and belief are part of human reality. Where people are now does not define them forever, and whatever choices they have made, your spiritual task is still to love them as God does.

5. When someone says things you disagree with or do not fully comprehend, turn to wonder: "I wonder why he feels this way?" "I wonder what brought her to this conclusion?" "I wonder why I am feeling this way as I listen to him?"[4]

6. You can learn to let God be the one who transforms what might need to be changed in another's life. This means letting go the arrogant assumption that you are here to save, fix, or change others into who or what you think they ought to be.

I would like to lift up three other spiritual practices that can be life changing for anyone having trouble in relationships. The first is what my colleague Jane Vennard calls "The Compassionate Observer."[5] The second is praying for those we have come to experience as "enemies." The third is practicing the craft of forgiveness.

The Compassionate Observer

Vennard reminds us that each of us has, deep inside, the capacity to see others—and ourselves—with the eyes of compassion. It is the "Christ center" or "true self" within us that sees this way. With a little intention and practice we can access it in our daily lives. What follows is my own adaptation of the process Vennard teaches, combined with insights from other spiritual teachers and my own experience.

When someone unexpectedly interrupts you or does something inappropriate, you need not simply react with the irritation that first rises up in you. Take a deep breath, step back inwardly, and name what you are feeling. Then take a second breath and go deeper inside. Instead of closing your heart, open it to the person who has offended or surprised you. Find the place of compassion within you that burns like a gentle flame. Feel the warmth of care and concern in this "heart of your heart." You can, through imagination, "feed the flame" with your breathing, just as airflow increases the intensity of a fire. Looking out from the eyes of compassion, can you discern some need or suffering or ignorance that lies behind the offending behavior? Let the compassion of Christ guide your spirit. Allow your response to the offending person, whether spoken aloud or in silent thought, come from this center.

You can also use this practice with yourself when you feel judgmental about your abilities, choices, or perceived weaknesses. For example, if you feel like a failure as a parent, or are ashamed over how you have treated your spouse, or suffer guilt for judging a friend unfairly, try this: sit quietly a while, moving into your deep soul-center, where Christ abides and love resides. Envision and feel the flame of compassion within. Feed this flame gently with each breath, and sense how the love within expands as you attend to it. When it feels full and strong, take two pieces of paper. On the first, write all the reasons you are, or could be, a good parent, spouse, or friend. On the other, write all the reasons you are not, or cannot be, a good parent, spouse, or friend. Then put one list on each knee, or on the desk or floor before you. Go back to the heart of compassion within and, if you need to, "feed the flame" again with your breathing until it is warm and full. Then look at each side of you from that place of compassion. Both sides of you have truth in them. What happens to your perception of your self when you look at each of these sides with compassion? When you complete this practice, it is helpful to write down what you see and learn in the process.

Interceding for Our Enemies

The second and related practice is praying for those we have difficulty loving. As Christians, we often don't wish to concede that we have enemies. Yet we all know the experience of feeling at enmity with others, even—perhaps particularly—with those closest to us. It has been said, and is true to my own experience, that we cannot continue to despise or hate a person for whom we regularly and sincerely pray. Here is a process that enlists our imagination to intercede for those we struggle to accept with love. If you choose to share it, copy and give it to others so they can review the basic process and engage it in their own time and way.

Imaging Intercession for Those Hard to Love

In using imagination to intercede for others, we are neither manipulating the Spirit of God nor the person we are praying for. We are simply opening our minds and hearts to envision with God's help the fullness of life, healing, cleansing, or renewal for another person. We are seeing, by God's grace, new possibilities for someone's life, leaving the specific work of transformation to the Spirit.

- Relax your body and mind; breathe deeply; release surface thoughts.

- Come into God's presence, imaging it as light. Jewish faith speaks of the *Shekinah*—the glory, radiance, or covering of God. Picture something of this glory.

- In God's presence we are not alone, but present with all who are held in the divine heart. Choose one of God's children who is hard for you to love.

- Express to God how you feel toward this person. Ask God to help you discover the full measure of your feelings and judgments.

- Release your feelings and judgments, allowing God to absorb them so they might be transformed into something life-giving. Ask to see how God sees this person.

- Imagine this person held in God's light and love, and be there yourself. Invite the Holy Spirit to be at work in both of you for healing and wholeness.

- Envision a state of joy and wholeness in this person, as if she or he were restored to the full beauty of God's image. Can you envision yourself this way, too?

- Ask God for the realization of such blessing for both of you. Thank God for the gift of love and its potential for the other person, for you, and for all people.

- Release this person to God's care with full

trust that the Spirit will carry this work of grace forward, into the next occasion of your prayer.

Practicing the Craft of Forgiveness

Finally, perhaps nothing goes to the heart of broken human relationships as profoundly as forgiveness. Henri Nouwen once wrote, "Forgiveness is the name of love practiced among people who love poorly.... That is the great work of love among the fellowship of the weak that is the human family."[6]

Indeed, as human beings we fall and fail in love more often than we find our freedom in it. Our churches are awash with people who have not learned how to receive or give forgiveness. Yet Christ continues to teach, model, and offer us the spiritual power of his freedom to love, despite our self-preoccupied resistance to new life.

If Jesus—hanging from an instrument of torture, shame, and death—can forgive the most abhorrent human cruelty, betrayal, denial, and mockery (before even a hint of contrition on our part), surely we who are united with him in baptism and Holy Communion can find *in him* the grace to forgive one another for offenses we commit against one another. Forgiving others is both our calling and privilege in Christ. We know that forgiveness frees the giver as well as the receiver. It is God's "win-win" solution to human sin!

I do not wish, however, to make light of human difficulties with forgiveness. Our pastoral task is to receive people's feelings without judgment, give them permission to express their heartache and hope, help them see where they may be stuck, and offer resources to take the next step on their journey into healing and maturity. Christians in particular may need explicit permission and encouragement to grieve, shout, and shake their fist at God, as our Jewish forebears never hesitated to do. We have been taught to be polite, even toward God, whereas what we need is to be real, especially with God. God is not offended or dishonored by our anger; God comprehends it more fully than we and is ready to help us understand it if we are willing.

You can gently encourage people to probe what lies beneath their resistance either to receiving or offering forgiveness: hurt, fear, anger, guilt, and pride are often knotted up together. To untangle them is an important step toward releasing pain into God's transforming love. In the process, people often begin to see clearly, perhaps for the first time, how many accumulated life experiences are hiding behind their reactions to a particular incident. The discovery that we are holding on to a lifetime of pain, fear, or fury never adequately processed is the beginning of a more conscious integration of our life's experience. This in turn leads toward greater wholeness and maturity.

Coming to the point where authentic forgiveness is possible is usually a process, one that cannot be rushed or forced. People cannot command themselves to forgive, nor should we ever command others to do so. Forgiveness is the fruit of coming to a deeper understanding of the human heart in all its complexity. It is the result of "getting a new mind"—the true meaning of repentance—which we understand as the mind of Christ. The capacity to forgive comes through that emotional and spiritual maturation process by which we grow toward the fullness of Christ.

Practical Steps and Spiritual Practices

When visiting those whose relational wounds suggest the need to forgive or to be forgiven, invite them to reflect on whether they feel ready to move toward forgiveness or feel a need for further preparation—perhaps clarifying what forgiveness is and is not; perhaps acknowledging their true feelings to themselves and to God. Individuals may feel unable to move forward because they are misunderstanding forgiveness in some way:

- Denying their real feelings, hoping that ignoring the pain will make it go away

- Taking inappropriate blame for the wounding behavior of others: "It's my fault I got hurt; I must have done something to deserve this."

- Putting others "on probation," waiting for evidence that they deserve forgiving (changed behavior or contrition may never come)

- Imagining that forgiveness would condone or excuse bad behavior (a simple distinction between person and behavior may be helpful here)

- Laboring under the mistaken notion that "to forgive is to forget," when deep traumas cannot be forgotten even if they can be forgiven

If a person seems stuck in one of these ways, you may be able to suggest alternative ways of understanding the nature of forgiveness. You can also offer a few simple practices to help people work through their painful feelings.

Praying with Psalms of Lament and Imprecation

One of the great, time-tested Christian practices is "praying the Psalms." This usually means meditating with the Psalter as given, chewing over the deep feelings expressed there, discovering how they echo or evoke our own emotions, and adding our heartfelt prayers to God through them. It can be helpful to look at several translations, particularly fresh ones that illumine perspectives we have not been attuned to when reading overly familiar words.

You can encourage people to turn to this ancient practice, helping them locate a few psalms that might connect with their situation. Psalms of lament and imprecation are perhaps most useful for those dealing with issues of forgiveness. *Lament* gives vent to grief, pain, yearning, and hope. *Imprecation* gives us permission even to ask God to rain down curses on our enemies! In Psalm 69 we hear the plaintive voice of both:

> You know full well the insults
>   I've received;
>   you know my shame and disgrace. (v. 19)

> Insults have broken my heart.
>   I'm sick about it.
> I hoped for sympathy,
>   but there wasn't any;
>   I hoped for comforters,
>   but couldn't find any.
> They gave me poison for food. (vv. 20-21a)

> Pour out your anger on them—
>   let your burning fury catch them. (v. 24)

Pile guilt on top of their guilt!…
Let them be wiped out
    of the scroll of life!…
And me? I'm afflicted.
    I'm full of pain.
Let your salvation keep me safe, God! (vv. 27-29)

Reading a psalm like this, we can be struck by how immature the sentiments are. It seems all complaint and blame, like a child railing to parents, demanding that they punish a wayward sibling. Yet these are often realistic feelings washing around inside us when we feel aggrieved or wounded. Where do we take them, if not to God?

You can suggest that people struggling with forgiveness write their own psalms, with the same inner freedom to express their heart to God that the ancient Jews had in writing and praying to theirs. People don't need to worry about whether their psalms mimic the form of traditional psalmody. This is essentially poetry from the heart, born of honest prayer. Writing our own psalms helps us get in touch with the full range of our feelings, to uncover their roots and knots, to see our inner conditions with greater clarity. As we express our rage, sadness, or despair to God in a personal psalm, we slowly begin to receive from the Spirit a sense of release, a gradual shift from the intensity of our pain as we let God absorb and transform our most negative feelings.

This is the one of the great gifts of praying the Psalms.

If those you are caring for seem ready to do the work of forgiveness, two simple spiritual practices can be very helpful depending on whether the need is to seek forgiveness or to offer it: writing a good apology and writing a letter of forgiveness. Here are the basics of each one.

Guidelines for Writing a Good Apology

- Be respectful of the person you are writing to, using courtesy and tact.
- Do not try to defend yourself, make excuses, or explain all the circumstances.
- Go right to the point, using simple, direct language.

Following these simple but demanding principles will result in a "clean, straightforward apology."[7]

Guidelines for Writing a Letter of Forgiveness

- Write a letter forgiving someone toward whom you feel resentment or deep disappointment. It could be someone you live or work with, a person who has already died, or even yourself. Who needs your forgiveness?

- Clarify the nature of the offensive behavior, and name the truth of your feelings—hurt, angry, shamed, grieved, betrayed. It may be helpful to put it in these terms: "When you did (or said)..., I felt..."

- State, in your own words, that you are choosing to let go of your resentment or desire to "pay back in kind." You are expressing a desire to release the offender from the alienating effect of the offense on your relationship.

A few general pointers in this process:

- Be aware that you cannot control another person's response. You are simply choosing to free yourself from the burden of this bondage to the past.

- Remember, God has empowered you to forgive as you have been forgiven in Christ. Ask for grace to let God take the burden from you, now and forever.

- You may decide to send this letter or not. Regardless, you can expect some movement forward and a new sense of energy to flow from this exercise.[8]

Working on forgiveness in these simple ways can be a source of great empowerment to people who have become stuck in painful relationships. The central Christian practice of forgiveness can heal broken hearts and reorient us to one another in ways that open up possibilities for a new future. Even relationships that we have long since despaired of can be restored if the gift of forgiveness is genuinely offered and received.

The free gift of forgiveness is precisely what God has offered us in Jesus. If we have any sense for what this gift means in our own lives, we will see why we are asked to share the gift with others. When we know ourselves to be loved and forgiven by God, we are less afraid to risk failure in our stumbling steps forward into the fullness of Christ. We begin to let go of our expectations of perfection—for others and for ourselves; we make more allowances for the false starts and fumbling of those around us; we become more tolerant of human inconsistencies; we see our own weaknesses reflected in the weakness of others, rather than projecting our inner darkness onto easy scapegoats. In other words, we become more humane, more mature, more loving.

Indeed, knowing ourselves as forgiven sinners is one of the greatest sources of encouragement on earth! It puts the heart back into us for the adventure and challenge of life. Whatever we can do as spiritual caregivers to help others move

toward this freedom will bring greater healing and integrity into our sorely wounded and
wounding world.

Prayers for Relational Encouragement

For a Parent-Child Relationship:
Gracious God, our Heavenly Parent,

You have created each one of us with a wise design
for our life,
> and you give us the gift of particular roles
> throughout our lives.

We trust that you know all there is to know about
being a parent,
> admitting that we are always learning what it
> means to become better parents.

Today we pray for your servant (name),
> thanking you for (his or her) desire and hope to
> express your love and truth
> in a way that honors and reflects your love for
> us in Jesus Christ.

Console (name) in (her or his) grief, pain, confusion,
fear, anger, and sadness.
May Jesus' example of healing grace, and truth spoken in love,
> guide (name) as (she or he) seeks a more Christ-
> like expression

of (her or his mothering or fathering) role with (name of child).

May your Holy Spirit fill (name) with the love only you can give.
And may (name of child) be open to receive your grace and guidance through (him or her).
We ask these things in the name of your Son, our Lord, Jesus Christ. Amen.

For a Couple's Relationship:

God of Wisdom and Love,

You have been present in drawing (name) and (name) together into a shared life.
You know the heart and need of both of them, more deeply than they know themselves.
We trust that the infinite treasury of your heart
> holds every gift needed to heal and strengthen the fabric of their love for each other.

Today we pray that both of them may seek the gifts they most need from you,
> to bring a stronger, truer, more durable love into their relationship.

Help each see what he or she lacks, and what you alone can supply.
Guide them into deeper emotional and spiritual maturity.
Help them practice seeing each other and themselves with your compassion.
Open their minds to the forgiving mind of Christ.

Lift and fill the heart of each, (name) and (name),
>with your truth, guidance, wisdom, generosity,
>and faithfulness;
for we know we cannot love each other as you love
us, apart from your grace.

We ask this in the name of him who shows us your
love with such clarity,
>Jesus Christ, our Lord. Amen.

For Estranged Friends:

O God, Truest Friend of our Souls,

You extended friendship to us in Jesus,
>who showed us that no one has greater love than
>to lay down life for a friend.

Teach us what it means today to lay down our lives
for a friend:
>perhaps to lay down self-centered motivations
>in our friendship,
>or to lay down unrealistic expectations,
>or to lay down our desire to control the relation-
>ship to our liking.

Teach us rather to listen more deeply to each other;
>to accept each other more truly;
>to speak truth with love;
>to offer support and encouragement with inner
>freedom;
>to receive critical words with greater humility;

to forgive, and to absorb forgiveness for ourselves;

to pray for each other.

May these spiritual gifts be your special grace to (name) and (name) this day.

In the name of the One who called his disciples to maturity as friends,

our great Teacher and Lord, Jesus Christ. Amen.

CHAPTER 4

The Courage to Grow in Intimacy with God

The God we come to know in Christ is the most astonishingly splendid Reality imaginable. Scripture reassures us of this truth repeatedly. God is Creator of everything known and unknown. "In the beginning" God recognizes and declares "good" all that is fashioned by divine power. God creates human beings in the divine image and likeness for a special intimacy with their Creator and a role of responsible stewardship for other creatures on earth. God calls us into covenant faithfulness, remaining faithful even when we don't keep up our end of the bargain: " 'If we are disloyal, he stays faithful' because he can't be anything else than what he is" (2 Tim. 2:13).

Divine faithfulness takes infinite expression. God repeatedly forgives human failing:

The Lord! The Lord!
a God merciful and gracious,
slow to anger,
and abounding in steadfast love and
    faithfulness. (Exod. 34:6 NRSV)

Our divine Parent receives us back after we run off to false gods—the gods of security, power, prestige, and pleasure, who cater to our egotistic needs—the gods the prodigal of Jesus' parable pursued and who so deeply penetrate our cultural values today. The Holy One offers us a way out of the death-dealing consequences of our sin: God, the Word, comes to us in human form to open a new way of salvation and healing for a profoundly immature, confused, and corrupted humanity. Even when we display our most deformed traits with Jesus—cynicism, betrayal, denial, false accusation, torture, and murder—he expresses God's eternally faithful, creative love by forgiving and lifting us to new possibilities of life. This is indeed good news!

Yet in our continued immaturity and brokenness, we can absorb only so much good news. We are adept at seeing our glass half empty rather than half full, so we easily get discouraged in our relationship with God. I have sat with the faithful and the lapsed alike, listening to many anguished confessions and questions.

Vignettes of God's Felt Absence

A chemical engineer in his late thirties did volunteer youth ministry in his twenties before getting married and moving to another state for a job. With deep sadness he acknowledges a growing estrangement in his soul: "I used to feel close to God. I studied the Bible, prayed frequently, and often felt the Lord's blessing and guidance in my life. But things have changed so much since then. I'm not sure quite when it started or why. It seems like work has taken over my life. The church my wife and I attended for a few years wasn't meeting my spiritual needs, and we had trouble finding one where we both felt at home. Maybe I'm too tired, or just getting jaded. I have so many more questions about Christian faith than I did when I was younger. I'm not satisfied by answers I used to trust—they seem so simplistic now. To be honest, God feels a million miles away. Sometimes I even wonder if God is for real."

A woman in her early fifties speaks to me wistfully: "My prayer life has become so unsatisfying. I used to know what to do to feel God's nearness, but now the ways I used to pray don't seem to work for me anymore. I feel lost. I've hit a wall and don't know how to break through it. I know God is there, but only by faith. I'm trusting in the dark. All my life, at every significant turn, I have relied on my relationship with God—so when I can't feel that presence or guidance, it's like a huge hole inside me."

The young woman beside me is agitated, rocking back and forth with a look of terrified anguish on her face. In a tone of desperation she whispers, "I know God has abandoned me. I'm sure I have committed the unpardonable sin—a sin against the Holy Spirit. God will not forgive me. He has withdrawn from my life, and I can't feel his assurance anymore. What shall I do?"

These glimpses of discouragement and anxiety in our relationship with God typify faith issues many of us struggle with. Most of us go through stretches where God feels absent, or at least distant. Life's changing circumstances can slowly move us away from earlier experiences of intimacy with God. Like the bewildered chemical engineer, we may have little idea how or why a feeling of God's absence has developed.

The painful trials and tragedies we inevitably encounter in life can so shake the foundations of our faith that we seriously wonder about the goodness, power, or even reality of God. Traumas like the untimely death of a child, a massive natural disaster, the devastating effects of war, or a shocking act of abuse in our community can thrust us into spiritual turmoil. It may seem impossible to imagine how God can be present in such things or what kind of God would be present in them.

At times life seems to dish out loss upon loss, obstacle after obstacle. Then we may feel not so much abandoned as actively *persecuted* by God. When multiple calamities struck Job, he famously expressed the sense of being pursued by a vindictive, punishing God:

> I will speak in the anguish
>   of my spirit;
> I will complain in the bitterness of my soul.
> . . . .
> When I say, 'My bed will comfort me,
>   my couch will ease my complaint,'
> then you scare me with dreams
>   and terrify me with visions,
> so that I would choose strangling
>   and death rather than this body.
> . . . .
> What are human beings, that you make so
>   much of them,
>   that you set your mind on them,
> visit them every morning,
>   test them every moment?
> Will you not look away from me for a while,
>   let me alone until I swallow my spittle?
> . . . .
> Why have you made me your target?
>   Why have I become a burden to you? (Job
> 7:11-20 NRSV)

Job never understood why he had become God's "target." At the end of his book, he is left (as are we) with no answer but the impenetrable mystery of divine will. The book does not give us a satisfactory reason for Job's suffering, just as we rarely receive satisfactory reasons for our own. The story sets us up to understand his misery as a form of testing, which may help us see our own suffering as a test of faith or trial of purification. Yet even those of us prepared to interpret our suffering this way struggle to understand why we should have to undergo such tests or trials.

At times we can trace some factors that have led us to feel distant from God. As with the chemical engineer, perhaps we have slowly stopped nourishing our spirits—ceasing to worship with a community, or pray regularly, or meditate on Scripture. When we allow our doubts to grow, apart from any conversation with persons or perspectives of faith, our spiritual growth can be arrested at an adolescent stage. Naturally, answers that sufficed in our youth may not stand the test of time. We need to bump up against questions, doubts, and new information in order to grow toward larger frames of meaning, more adequate understandings of reality. But this doesn't mean casting away the whole enterprise of faith. There are always broader interpretations, more encompassing perspectives that can speak to our doubts and fears. If we are seeking, the Spirit will bring "teachers" into our lives when we are ready to hear them.

For some, as turned out to be the case with the despairing young woman, our early life has taught us that parents are not trustworthy. When life gets rough we expect God, the Supreme Parent, to abandon us also. Perhaps, like that young woman, we have done something we believe to be profoundly displeasing to God, and our guilt has driven us far from a sense of divine presence. Then it is only a small step to convince ourselves that we are condemned beyond all possibility of redemption.

The felt absence of God is a painful and frightening experience for anyone who has felt strongly connected to God's presence in the past. It constitutes a lost sense of relationship—with one not simply like our selves, but rather who stands as the source of our being and meaning. This sense of loss was clear in the situation of the woman who no longer knew how to pray.

Praying the Psalms, Again

As a spiritual caregiver, you can help people understand this sense of loss as a common experience—part of the fallen human condition of estrangement from God. It surfaces across boundaries of time and culture. The ancient Jews struggled with this sense of God's withdrawal and rejection as much as anyone today: "Why do you reject my very being, LORD? / Why do you hide your face from me?" (Ps. 88:14). Waiting for God to reappear in one's life has long been part of the human struggle: "I am tired of crying....My eyes are exhausted / with waiting for my God" (Ps. 69:3).

We have mentioned that one of the most helpful practices is writing our own psalms of lament, expressing fully and freely to God all that is in our heart. This practice often puts us in touch with the deeper reservoir of our faith and hope. Like so many psalms that turn on a dime from despair to assured affirmations of faith, once we have emptied our hearts of complaint and vented our pain we may recognize a bedrock of hope that allows us to continue entrusting ourselves to divine care and guidance.

Here is the lovely paradox: psalms that wonder aloud where on earth God has gone nonetheless presume God's reality. Even if we are lamenting a profound sense of divine absence, we are still expressing a relationship with God through prayer itself. Therefore we can affirm a deeper trust in the One we cannot see, feel, or know in all the ways we might like to. This truth brings us to the faith experience sometimes called the "dark night of the soul" on our journey into Christ.

The Dark Night Experience

The phrase "dark night of the soul" comes from the remarkable spiritual poetry of John of the Cross, a sixteenth-century Spanish mystic. But the experience he evokes by this phrase is essentially a "Rubicon" every Christian serious about spiritual growth must cross over. Father Thomas Keating, founder of the Centering Prayer Movement, calls it the "crisis of faith" that comes to every person who is truly maturing in Christ. Just as in successful human maturation we grow out of overdependence on our parents' world-view and authority, discovering instead our own views and inner authority, so God calls us out of immature to mature expressions of faith.

In spiritual terms, this means losing our worldly idea of "self" in order to discover our true self in God. The process requires that we be deprived of the ordinary ways we have known divine presence and comfort in earlier stages of our spiritual journey. This was the experience of the woman who no longer knew how to pray. She was in her spiritual "midlife crisis." The ways she used to pray didn't work for her now; she still had faith, but a faith held in darkness.

The weaker our faith, the more we require some kind of sensible presence of God to accompany our prayer: a sense of assurance; a feeling of peace; the warmth of love; a clear insight or "word from the Lord." In our spiritual infancy we love God for the gifts we receive in our relationship. As we grow up into Christ, God gives us opportunities to "increase our faith" (Luke 17:5). As Keating writes: "The absence of the felt presence of The Lord is his normal means of increasing our faith and of getting us to the point of believing in the power of his word alone...without the feeling of his presence or external props."[1]

If in your caregiving relationships you encounter persons who cannot find solace in their earlier way of praying, you can offer several encouragements. First, let them know that a sense of deprivation can be normal at certain stages of spiritual growth. This gives people confidence that they are neither isolated in their experience nor praying in the wrong way, which many fear. Second, help them see it as an invitation from God toward a deeper level of intimacy, one that does not depend on felt experiences of divine presence. The great saints and spiritual writers suggest God is weaning them away from dependence on sensible consolations, opening up the possibility of a deeper union that comes by "naked faith"—trust in God's presence and continued work in the hidden depths of the soul. In drawing us beyond our ordinary ways of knowing divine presence, God teaches us to love God for who God is, not merely for what God does for us.

Simply learning that their experience of prayer is not abnormal and has a constructive purpose can be enormously hopeful for persons grieving the loss of their accustomed forms of intimacy with God. It is one way of dying to the old and opening to the new life God would give us.

Many confuse "dark night of the soul" with any form of spiritual distress, or even with depression. The phrase has come to serve as a powerful metaphor for any kind of painful constraints in matters of our inner life. But in Christian tradition, this phrase carries the more specific meaning described here. Spiritual dryness is generally another matter, referring to the boredom of a regular prayer pattern or the inner drought caused by falling away from regular sustenance in spiritual practice. Perseverance in prayer is the recommended cure for the first, and restoration of regular prayer practice is the remedy for the second. But if one is persevering in a regular practice where faith remains alive but the experience of God's presence is unrecognizable, or the familiar avenues of prayer seem to bring one to an impenetrable impasse, a true "dark night" is likely the case. In this situation, encourage people to wait with love, continued faith, and deep attention to how the Spirit will lead them through the impasse to a new way of knowing God.

The God Who Suffers with Us

You may also be able to help people recognize that, spiritually speaking, God *cannot* be absent from us. God is present everywhere at all times, according to the very nature of divine being. South African pastor Trevor Hudson lifts up a text from Ephesians 4:6, which assures us of "one God and Father of all who is over all, through all, and in all." He writes: "There is no fear, no loss, no grief, no loneliness, no despair, no addiction, no desolation, no suffering that God does not share in. God is continually present and reaching out to us in whatever we may be going through at this moment."[2]

Although this is spiritually true, we can certainly *feel* as if God is absent, and therefore experience the pain and fear that come with a sense of abandonment or rejection. Even Jesus knew the heart-sickening horror of feeling God's abandonment. He whose life was so intimately bound to his heavenly Father's—who received words, guidance, and power from God for each step of his ministry—cries out on the cross, "My God, my God, why have you forsaken me?" (Matt. 27:46, NRSV). Near the end of his physical endurance, he loses his lifelong experience of personal union with God. This is part of the incomparable spiritual suffering of Jesus, as he descends fully into the alienated consequence of human sin. Surely it is a comfort to Christians that Jesus knew from experience the anguish of losing all sense of divine presence. He participates in every form of our suffering. As the Letter to the Hebrews says: "We don't have a high priest who can't sympathize with our weaknesses but instead one who was tempted in every way that we are, except without sin….Although he was a Son, he learned obedience from what he suffered" (4:15; 5:8).

A profound spiritual practice for Christians in the midst of suffering is to meditate on the cross— not the empty cross of most Protestant sanctuaries but the "crucifix" on which we behold Jesus suffering as we suffer. This can be done with the physical aid of a crucifix, an icon or painting of Jesus on the cross, or simply in the mind's eye. For some, visual aids are deeply helpful, while for others imagination is the best way to access a sense of God's presence in prayer.

Exploring Our Images of God

There are some whose notion of deity is not large enough to permit God to participate in human suffering. They imagine God to be beyond what belongs to the lot of earthly creatures subject to sin and death. Yet this is not the picture we receive from the cross. In his passion, Jesus shows us the face of God fully immersed in human suffering for the sake of our healing and salvation.

As people mature in faith, they discover ways in which their image of God has been inadequate. Some are afraid that God cannot handle their strongest feelings, implying that their deity is not robust enough for life in the real world. Others feel a need to protect God's reputation, as if God somehow needed human protection. Douglas Steere once quipped that God is far less squeamish than his theological bodyguard![3] Many people entertain an image of the deity primarily as a disapproving, punishing judge. When they experience more kindness and mercy from others than they expect from God, they may begin to see how small and pinched their image of God truly is. Some can only imagine God as masculine; if "the voice of the Lord" they hear in Scripture is always deep, commanding, and tinged with authoritarianism, their God-image is clearly shaped by a limited human experience of male gender. As we outgrow childhood ideas that no longer fit our sense of reality, we may be unsure of what takes their place. What would a mature image of God be like? This is a wonderful challenge to explore!

In the role of spiritual caregiving, there may be occasions when you can help others explore their God-images. Here are questions you might find helpful at various times for inviting others to ponder or reconsider their notions about God:[4]

- Do you believe God actively wills calamity, disaster, or trauma?

- When difficult, painful circumstances arise in your life, do you think God is punishing you for something you did wrong?

- If you do something wrong, do you believe God loves you less? Or if you drift away from God, do you think God will be reluctant to let you come close again?

- Do you think evil is sometimes more powerful than God?

- How "masculine" is God in your view, and what characteristics do you associate with masculinity? What "feminine" traits of God can you recognize, and how do they affect your image of what is divine?

- What are you most afraid of in your relationship with God?

- What do you most desire or hope for in your relationship with God?

Images of God are deeply internalized and often subconscious. It takes time to shift our mental pictures, yet ideas about God will continue to change throughout our lives if we are open to continued spiritual growth. God is always beyond whatever notions we have of divine being; we can never fully capture God's reality through our limited reason or experience.

In your caregiving role, you can encourage people to look at God through the lens of Jesus: Given the way he prays, teaches, heals, and relates to others (especially outcasts and sinners), how do you imagine he sees his *Abba*? How do his life, death, and resurrection show us the nature of God? Grasping that God-in-Christ suffers with us is a great source of comfort and peace to most Christians. It reassures them there is no situation we can undergo in life from which God is ever absent.

You can also offer Scripture texts that illumine the loving presence of God. For those in the midst of trouble, including those who fear God has abandoned them or departed from them, focus on the promise of God's constant presence:

I won't desert you or leave you. Be brave and strong. (Josh. 1:5-6)

When you pass through the waters, I will be
    with you;
    and through the rivers, they shall not
        overwhelm you. (Isa. 43:2 NRSV)

Even when I walk
    through the darkest valley,
    I fear no danger
        because you are with me. (Ps. 23:4)

Where could I go to get away
    from your spirit?
    Where could I go to escape
        your presence?
If I went up to heaven,
    you would be there.
    If I went down to the grave,
        you would be there too....
If I said,
    "The darkness will definitely hide me;
    the light will become night around me,"
even then the darkness
    isn't too dark for you!
    Nighttime would shine bright as day
    because darkness is the same
        as light to you! (Ps. 139:7-8, 11-12)

I won't leave you as orphans. I will come to
you.... The Companion, the Holy Spirit, whom
the Father will send in my name, will teach you
everything and will remind you of everything I
told you. (John 14:18, 26)

And remember, I am with you always, to the end
of the age. (Matt. 28:20 NRSV)

A wise bishop writes, "When the worst happens God doesn't promise us an answer; God provides us a relationship."[5] God is not simply present, but present with active care and concern for our well-being. A series of parables in Luke 15 offers supporting evidence that God is deeply interested in each one of us, even—maybe particularly—when we have strayed or erred in life. The parable of the lost sheep suggests that, like a good shepherd, God seeks us out when we have strayed from the safety of the flock not so much by intention as by distraction. We can easily "nibble our way lost," focusing on the tasty tufts of grass before us, moving from one attractive bit of turf to another, until we discover we are not where we meant to be.

The final parable in this chapter is especially powerful. It shows that God's patient, active, yearning love for us applies equally when we willfully rebel and purposely reject our true home in God. The prodigal son does not slowly drift away from this father's house by incremental distraction, like a lost sheep; he rudely dishonors his father, flees as far as he can, and flings himself into a life of wasted morals as determinedly as possible. Even toward such rebellion, God shows the divine nature of long-suffering love. God takes that initiative called *grace* and pours it liberally on the child who returns.

The Living Parable of Jesus

These parables can be deeply encouraging to those who feel they have failed or disappointed God. Yet the greatest parable is Jesus' life. His passion, death, and resurrection constitute the clearest evidence of God's forgiving, restoring love. So we return to the central Christian theme of forgiveness, this time focused more on our relationship with God than with others, though they are hard to separate.

In his living parable, Jesus does not wait for repentance. As soon as he is crucified—even before the soldiers have cast lots for his clothing—Jesus prays, "Father, forgive them, for they don't know what they're doing" (Luke 23:34). He wants to forgive those who do not yet know how desperately they need forgiveness. A single sentence in Romans sheds light on why God might choose to offer forgiveness before we know we need it: "Do you not realize that God's kindness is meant to *lead you* to repentance?" (2:4b NRSV, emphasis added).

Scholar Gregory Jones suggests that the relationship between forgiveness and repentance is not necessarily what we have imagined: namely that repentance is the unalterable condition for forgiveness. Repentance before forgiveness is surely the norm. But Jesus reveals a dimension of

mercy that transcends the norm. In Jones's view
it is this: repentance is necessary to forgiveness
not as a prerequisite but as the only adequate response.[6] Peter Storey, former bishop of the Johan-
nesburg/Soweto area, agrees. He puts it this way:
"For us to be made right with God, repentance is
always necessary, but repentance is not so much
a condition for forgiveness as a consequence of
it.... We repent because we discover...how much
we have been forgiven."[7] Of course, if God's
mercy does *not* result in our sincere, full-hearted
repentance, it shows that we have neither understood nor appropriated the gift.

To people who fear that what they have done
is beyond God's help, the divine initiative and
desire to forgive can be a deeply freeing perspective. It is echoed in a tender story found among
the "sayings" of the early desert fathers and
mothers: "An elder was asked by a certain soldier if God would forgive a sinner. And he said
to him: Tell me, beloved, if your cloak is torn, will
you throw it away? The soldier replied and said:
No. I will mend it and put it back on. The elder
said to him: If you take care of your cloak, will
God not be merciful to His own image?"[8] Simple
wisdom like this can sometimes break through
foolish human fears. This story helps us recognize that divine mercy must at least amount to
more than we are capable of showing ourselves
(or our possessions!). Yet our twisted inner logic,

often unconscious, can convince us that we are too bad even for God to forgive! To hold God's mercy hostage to a determination to punish ourselves is truly a human sickness of spirit.

You can encourage those who fear divine wrath to see the outstretched arms of Jesus on the cross as a sign of God's grace, extended before we know we need it. Once we know our need of forgiveness, our task is to accept the gift by turning our minds and hearts back to God. Again, this reorienting of our lives toward God is the meaning of repentance. You might help persons ponder what it would look like to turn their lives around in relation to whatever they feel unforgiven for. It might look like seeing God in a new light, or recognizing the value of their humanity in God's eyes. Depending on the situation, apology or making restitution to another might play an important role as well.

The Practice of Gratitude

In relation to our growing intimacy with God, I wish to lift up one last (not least) spiritual practice: cultivating gratitude in all circumstances. This is one of the most important expressions of life in Christ: "Rejoice always. Pray continually. Give thanks in every situation because this is God's will for you in Christ Jesus" (1 Thess. 5:16-18).

Even in our most distressing and difficult experiences—indeed, precisely within them—we can learn to thank God for all that is given to us. Practicing gratitude honors God and simultaneously serves our spiritual growth.

Gratitude opens our eyes to the very real blessings that always reside somewhere within and around difficult circumstances. We begin to recognize how God is present with us in the midst of suffering and confusion. Blessings are often "hidden in plain sight"—found in family, friends, neighbors, and even strangers who reach out with care and support; discovered in small comforts we take for granted; noticed in the abundant gifts of the natural world around us; discovered in our own hearts.

Practicing gratitude also opens us to possibilities and potentials that seem completely closed when we are focused on our pain. Recognizing what we are grateful for allows us to see where hope and joy lie; these in turn help us trust more deeply God's good will for our future, both in and beyond this world. In the daily practice of gratitude, we discover just how much we have to be grateful for.

You may be able to help people shift their focus from pain, disappointment, and grief to where and how God is present with them. If they seem open to conversation, ask simple questions like these:

- Where does a sense of hope live inside you? What is your deepest hope?

- In what or whom do you trust right now? How is this trust evident to you?

- Is there an aspect of goodness you can identify in your situation or condition?

- How is this experience causing you to grow or reevaluate some part of your life?

- Where is God "in the midst" of your experience?

Of course, timing is crucial when considering such questions. Use common sense and ask yourself what would be helpful if you were in the other person's shoes. For someone reeling from a fresh loss or wound, questions like these are premature. Those newly faced with crisis need time to process their experience before they can step back and find the larger perspective suggested by questions like these. Yet when basic feelings of grief, fear, and anger have been worked through to some degree, mulling over bigger questions can help people start to recover. Any recovery of faith, hope, and love allows people to rebuild life's meaning more centrally around the reality of God.

The seeds of hope and sense of life-purpose are planted deep within our souls by divine design. They are buried treasures to be discovered and nourished with a little digging and perseverance. Caregivers are like gardeners who trust the life deep down in others, encouraging them to find their own green thumb. May you find joy in cultivating your inner gardener for the sake of others, and may it draw you deeper into your own experience of Christ's love!

Prayer

Holy One, Life-giver, Soul-lover,

How grateful we are that you are our God:
> You have created us for a depth of communion with you that we can scarcely imagine;
> you have fashioned us in your own image for a high calling we have not yet fathomed;
> you love us so dearly and fiercely that we can never fall beneath your everlasting arms.

Yet we fall away from your love; in the maze of our human explorations and experiences we come to know fear, doubt, incomprehension, pain, and anger in our relationship with you. At times we withdraw, resist, or even reject and deny you. Yet you understand our wandering, our grief, our anger, and our pain. You remain faithful to us, with patience and endurance beyond our understanding. Your forgiveness is always available to us, if we will simply acknowledge our need and receive it.

O God of Grace, expand our images of you; enlarge our hearts to receive your love; open our eyes to see more clearly your presence in our lives. May our gratitude increase and overflow in joy and hope, faith and love, as we allow you to draw us closer to your heart. For you have made us for yourself, and our hearts are unfulfilled until you fill us with your love.

We pray in the name of him who shows us your gracious nature with such clarity—Jesus our Lord. Amen.

EMOTIONAL HEALTH
SELF-ASSESSMENT

Emotional Infancy
- Want others to care for us and see others as objects to meet our needs
- Driven by need for instant gratification
- Have difficulty entering another person's world

Emotional Childhood
- Content when we get what we want; complain, withdraw, manipulate, seek revenge, and get sarcastic when we don't get our way
- Easily hurt, and take disagreement as a personal offense
- Unravel with stress, disappointment, or trials
- Have difficulty discussing our needs and wants clearly and calmly

Emotional Adolescence
- Preoccupied with ourselves

- Threatened by criticism and tend to be defensive
- Critical and judgmental
- Have difficulty truly hearing another's pain, disappointment, or needs
- Deal poorly with conflict, often blaming, appeasing, or pouting; going to a third party; or ignoring the problem
- Keep tabs on what we give so we can later ask for something in return

Emotional Adulthood
- Ask clearly and honestly for what we need, want, or prefer
- Recognize, manage, and take responsibility for our own thoughts and feelings
- State our own beliefs and values without becoming adversarial
- Respect others without having to change them
- Give people room to make mistakes, not expecting perfection
- Appreciate persons for who they are, not for what they give back
- Accurately assess our own limits, strengths, and weaknesses, and freely discuss them with others

- Enter the feelings, needs, and concerns of others without losing ourselves
- Resolve conflict and negotiate solutions that take account of others' perspectives

Questions for Reflection

- In what ways do I express the characteristics of these stages?
- Which stages seem most dominant in my life?
- How do my less-mature characteristics affect my important relationships?
- Do certain relationships in my life elicit one stage more than another? Why?
- What specific steps might I take to grow into greater emotional maturity?
- Who can best help me with this process?

NOTES

Introduction

1. Julian of Norwich, *Showings: The Classics of Western Spirituality* (New York: Paulist Press, 1978), 315.

2. Attributed to St. John of Kronstadt. See http://orthodoxwiki.org/John_of_Kronstadt.

3. Thomas Keating, *The Mystery of Christ: Liturgy as Spiritual Experience* (New York: Continuum, 2008), 87.

4. Julian of Norwich, *Showings*, 225.

1. The Courage of Authentic Self-love

1. L. William Countryman, *Forgiven and Forgiving* (Harrisburg, PA: Morehouse Publishing, 1998), 29.

2. Douglas Steere, *Gleanings: A Random Harvest* (Nashville: Upper Room Books, 1986), 83.

3. See my book, *Soul Feast: An Invitation to the Christian Spiritual Life* (Louisville: Westminster John Knox Press, 1995; 2005), 46–47; 49, 50.

2. The Courage to Work from One's Center

1. This language is borrowed from Parker J. Palmer and the Center for Courage & Renewal. "Courage Work," as they call it, is described in Palmer's book *A*

Hidden Wholeness (San Francisco: Jossey-Bass, 2004). I highly recommend this resource in relation to the topic of this chapter.

2. Henri Nouwen, *Bread for the Journey* (San Francisco: HarperOne, 2006), 185.

3. The concept of open, honest questions is described in *A Hidden Wholeness*, chapter 8, and is taught to prepare people for the communal Quaker discernment practice called the "Clearness Committee."

4. See *A Hidden Wholeness*, chapter 4, especially the section titled "The Soul Is Shy."

5. Wayne Muller, *Sabbath: Restoring the Sacred Rhythm of Rest* (New York: Bantam Books, 1999), 70.

6. In addition to traditional vocational gifts inventories, there are several helpful spiritual gifts inventories you can point to. See *Revolutionizing Christian Stewardship for the 21st Century* by Dan Dick (Nashville: Discipleship Resources, 1997), 97–101, for a list of spiritual gifts. Another resource, by Charles V. Bryant, is titled *Rediscovering Our Spiritual Gifts* (Nashville: Upper Room Books, 1998).

3. The Courage to Grow in Relationships

1. Attributed to Saint Augustine, possibly a paraphrase of his ideas.

2. See Richard Rohr, *Falling Upward: A Spirituality for the Two Halves of Life* (San Francisco: Jossey-Bass, 2011).

3. Adapted from Peter Scazzero's realistic and helpful book *Emotionally Healthy Spirituality* (Nashville: Thomas Nelson, 2006), 178–79.

4. I owe this practice to Parker Palmer, who articulates it as one of the "Touchstones" in the Center

for Courage and Renewal's Circles of Trust, based on Palmer's *Healing the Heart of Democracy: The Courage to Create a Politics Worthy of the Human Spirit* (San Francisco: Jossey-Bass, 2011).

5. I first learned this practice in a workshop Jane led for a Pathways Conference held at The Upper Room in the late 1990s. She has also written about it, notably in her book *A Praying Congregation: The Art of Teaching Spiritual Practice* (Herndon, VA: The Alban Institute, 2005), 99–100.

6. Henri Nouwen, "Forgiveness: The Name of Love in a Wounded World," *Weavings*, vii, no. 2 (1992): 15.

7. Slightly adapted from my book *Companions in Christ: The Way of Forgiveness*, Participant's Book (Nashville: Upper Room Books, 2002), 92.

8. Revised from ibid., 80.

4. The Courage to Grow in Intimacy with God

1. Thomas Keating, *Crisis of Faith, Crisis of Love* (New York: Continuum, 1995), 16.

2. Trevor Hudson, *The Serenity Prayer* (Nashville: Upper Room Books, 2012), 75.

3. See Douglas Steere, *Dimensions of Prayer* (New York: Women's Division, Board of Global Ministries, United Methodist Church, 1962), 69. Steere's book was revised and republished by Upper Room Books in 1997.

4. Several of these are adapted from Trevor Hudson's book *The Serenity Prayer*, 91.

5. Robert Schnase, *Forty Days of Fruitful Living: Practicing a Life of Grace* (Nashville: Abingdon Press, 2010), 55. Several of the insights from Luke 15 paraphrased here are his.

6. See L. Gregory Jones, *Embodying Forgiveness: A Theological Analysis* (Grand Rapids: Eerdmans, 1995), especially chapter 4, 110, 121.

7. Peter Storey, *Listening at Golgotha* (Nashville: Upper Room Books, 2004), 34–35.

8. Thomas Merton, *The Wisdom of the Desert* (New York: New Directions, 1960), 76.

ABOUT THE AUTHOR

Marjorie J. Thompson, an ordained minister of the Presbyterian Church (USA), is a widely recognized spiritual formation teacher, retreat leader, and writer. She received her Bachelor of Arts in religious studies from Swarthmore College and her Master of Divinity from McCormick Theological Seminary. Following a post-graduate pastoral internship, she became a Research Fellow at Yale Divinity School where she studied Christian spirituality with Henri Nouwen and did independent research in ecumenical traditions of prayer.

Rev. Thompson began her ministry as an Associate Pastor for adult education and small group life at the First Presbyterian Church of Stamford, Connecticut. Over the years, she has served as adjunct faculty for numerous seminaries including McCormick, Wesley, Columbia, San Francisco, and Vanderbilt Divinity School. For a period she directed the foundations program for Stillpoint (Programs in Spiritual Direction and Contemplative Prayer) in Nashville. Marjorie has been a faculty presenter in The Upper Room's Academy for Spiritual Formation from its early years, a role she continues to enjoy.

For 12 years Marjorie worked on the staff of Upper Room Ministries as Director of the Pathways Center for Spiritual Leadership, later called Pathways in Congregational Spirituality. There she served as chief architect of a broadly acclaimed resource in small group spiritual formation, *Companions in Christ*. She authored several volumes in the Companions series.

Rev. Thompson is also the author of *Family: The Forming Center* and *Soul Feast: An Invitation to the Christian Spiritual Life*. Her writings have appeared in *Weavings, Worship, Upper Room Disciplines*, and *The Abingdon Preacher's Annual*. Recently she contributed a chapter to *A Spiritual Life: Perspectives from Poets, Prophets, and Preachers*, where she writes of her own spiritual practice.

Marjorie continues her ministry of teaching, writing, and retreat work under the banner of Transforming Practice Ministries.